New Elementary
MATHEMATICS

SYLLABUS D

WORKBOOK

Stein Valley Nlakapamux School
PO Bag 300, Lytton, BC, V0K 1Z0
Phone:(250) 455-2522 Fax:(250) 455-2512

Low Wai Cheng
B. Sc., Dip. E

D1119669

SNP
Panpac

An imprint of SNP Panpac Pte Ltd

SNP Panpac Pte Ltd
97 Ubi Avenue 4
Singapore 408754
Tel no   : (65) 6754 1993
Fax no   : (65) 6745 4129
Email   : panpmktg@snpcorp.com
Website : http://www.snpcorp.com
             http://www.snplearning.com

For enquiries, please contact the publisher.

First published 1999
Reprinted 2000
Reprinted 2001 (twice)
Reprinted 2003
Reprinted 2004
Reprinted 2005 (twice)

ISBN 981-208-531-9

Printed in Singapore by Utopia Press Pte Ltd

PREFACE

New Elementary Mathematics Workbook 1, a supplement to the textbook *New Elementary Mathematics 1*, is specially written to provide students with additional practice. It follows closely the latest Mathematics Syllabus for Lower Secondary Schools issued by the Ministry of Education, Singapore for use from 1992. Students are required to apply mathematical concepts to real-life problems.

Each *Revision Exercise* covers a chapter in the textbook and attempts have been made to integrate the appropriate concepts of different topics into a single question. *Test Papers* are provided after every two revision exercises to help reinforce concepts learnt. *Mid-Term* and *Final Term Assessment Papers* have also been included to prepare students for the final examination.

CONTENTS

CHAPTER 1 / Whole Numbers

1. **(a)** Evaluate $513 - 8 \times 9$.
    (b) Find the remainder when 612 is divided by 26.

2. Evaluate $\{[(46 + 28) \times 2 + 6] - 56 \div 7\} - 17$.

3. Evaluate $19 - 6 + 52 \div (4 + 9)$.

4. Evaluate the following:
    (a) $[(56 + 27) \times 3 + 8] - 17$ **(b)** $[(63 \div 7) + (48 \div 8)] \times 3$
    (c) $[(100 \div 5 + 6) \times 4] - 20$ **(d)** $39 - 4 + 78 \div (4 + 9)$
    (e) $723 - (8 \times 9 + 16)$

5. **(a)** Write down the number 'twenty thousand six hundred and three' in figures.
    (b) Write down the number '24 065' in words.

6. List all the factors of each of the following:
    (a) 18   **(b)** 30
    (c) 48   **(d)** 72

7. **(a)** Express 5 040 as a product of its prime factors using index notation.
    (b) What is the largest prime number that is a factor of 5 040?

8. From the set of numbers 9, 16, 23, 30, 37, 42, 49, 56, 63,
    (a) write down two prime numbers and find their product,
    (b) write down three square numbers and find their sum.

9. **(a)** Find all the prime numbers which are factors of 4 920.
    (b) Find the sum of all these numbers.

10. **(a)** Express 7 524 as a product of prime factors.
    (b) Find the sum of the prime factors.

11. **(a)** Express 1 584 as a product of prime factors.
    (b) What is the greatest prime factor of 1 584?

12. Express 9 000 as a product of its prime factors.

13. Express each of the following as a product of prime factors and give your answer in index notation.
   (a) 14
   (b) 26
   (c) 32
   (d) 45
   (e) 56
   (f) 68
   (g) 74
   (h) 136
   (i) 200
   (j) 365

14. Find the largest prime number less than:
   (a) 27
   (b) 45
   (c) 70
   (d) 250

15. (a) How many prime numbers are there between 10 and 40?
   (b) Find all the prime numbers between 150 and 170.

16. Find the prime factorisation of:
   (a) 288
   (b) 435

17. Find the HCF of:
   (a) 84, 378
   (b) 144, 240

18. Find the HCF of:
   (a) 120, 60, 45
   (b) $6a^2bc^3$, $9ac^2$, $12a^3b^2c$

19. Find the HCF of:
   (a) 63, 819
   (b) 169, 2 197

20. Find the LCM of:
   (a) 27 and 48
   (b) $4p^3qr^2$ and $72p^2r^3$

21. Find the LCM of each of the following sets of numbers.
   (a) 2, 8, 17
   (b) 6, 9, 18
   (c) 20, 25, 40
   (d) 16, 24, 36
   (e) 9, 15, 45

22. Find the HCF and LCM of $25x^2y^3z^5$ and $125xyz^3$.

23. If $4\,900 = 2^x \times 5^y \times 7^z$, find the values of x, y and z.

CHAPTER 2

Fractions, Decimals and Approximations

1. Simplify $\dfrac{4\frac{1}{2} + \frac{2}{3}}{\frac{8}{13} \times 4\frac{1}{3}}$.

2. Arrange $\dfrac{11}{12}, \dfrac{5}{8}, \dfrac{4}{15}$ in ascending order.

3. Evaluate $[(1\frac{5}{7} - 4\frac{2}{3}) \div 4\frac{3}{7}] - 8$.

4. Find the average of $\dfrac{3}{8}, \dfrac{1}{4}$ and $\dfrac{2}{5}$.

5. Express $\dfrac{7 - 1\frac{2}{3}}{2 + 1\frac{5}{9}}$ as a single fraction in its lowest terms.

6. Evaluate the following, giving your answers in their simplest form:

    (a) $\dfrac{1}{2} + \dfrac{1}{4} + \dfrac{1}{8}$

    (b) $2 \times \dfrac{22}{7} \times \dfrac{21}{4}$

    (c) $\left(2\frac{1}{4} + 3\frac{1}{2}\right) \div \dfrac{1}{8}$

    (d) $\dfrac{4}{5} - \dfrac{1}{2}$

7. Evaluate:
    (a) $26.5 + 13.35 + 47.2$

    (b) $43.7 - 5.81$

8. Evaluate:
    (a) $3.14 \times 16 \times 2$

    (b) $38.5 \div 11$

9. Evaluate:
    (a) $0.7 \times 0.6 \times 0.3$

    (b) $27 \div 0.9$

10. Evaluate:
    (a) $5 \times (2 + 0.2) - 4 \div 16$

    (b) 0.8×0.9

    (c) $5.8 + 6.2 \times 0.2$

11. Round off the following correct to
    (i)   the nearest whole number,
    (ii) 1 decimal place,
    (iii) 3 decimal places.
    (a)   58.234 68   (b)   39.592 83
    (c)   63.724 56   (d)   88.329 43

12. Evaluate $8.3 \times 20.8 - \left(\dfrac{4.8}{0.3}\right)$.

13. The following table shows the amount of money a boy spends on sweets and comics in a week.

Item	Amount
Sweets	$0.45
Comics	$1.52

    Calculate how much the boy spends in 18 weeks, giving your answer in dollars and cents.

14. (a) Evaluate $2.5^2 - 2.4 \times 0.8$.
    (b) Find the number which when divided by 0.024 gives an exact answer of 1.9.

15. Given that 1 litre = 0.22 gallons, find the number of litres in 2 gallons, giving your answer correct to 2 decimal places.

16. Evaluate the following and correct your answers to 2 decimal places.
    (a) $\dfrac{1.86 - 2.01}{15.27 + (-15)}$ (b) $\dfrac{0.113 \times 0.315}{0.9 \times 0.05} \div 0.03$

17. Evaluate $60 - \dfrac{1}{2}[3 \times 5 - (105 \div 5 + 6 \times 2)]$.

18. Use your calculator to complete the following, giving your answers correct to 3 decimal places.
    $$\frac{15.7 \times 1.8}{5.9} = \frac{}{5.9} =$$

19. Using a calculator, evaluate $59.2 - 1.2 \times 0.12 + 5.078$, correct to 3 significant figures.

20. (a) Express 0.005 378 correct to 3 significant figures.
    (b) Express 56.238 correct to 1 decimal place.
    (c) Evaluate 35.8×5.2 and express your answer to 2 significant figures.

4

21. Using a calculator, evaluate $\dfrac{1}{4.56} - \dfrac{1}{7.2}$, correct to 3 significant figures.

22. Use a calculator to evaluate $\dfrac{27.2 + 7.31}{8.6 \times 5.9} + \dfrac{1.23 \times 2.6}{7.1 - 5.3}$ correct to 3 significant figures.

23. (a) Evaluate $\left(2.8 + \dfrac{2.7}{0.3}\right) \div \dfrac{0.64}{0.8}$ and correct your answer to 1 decimal place.

(b) Express $\dfrac{324}{56}$ as a decimal and round off your answer to 3 significant figures.

24. (a) Express $\dfrac{9}{4} + \dfrac{5}{8}$ as a decimal.

(b) Calculate the exact value of $53.312 \div 0.003\,4$.

25. Evaluate the following and leave your answers as fractions.

(a) $\dfrac{6\frac{1}{4} \div 3\frac{1}{2}}{5\frac{1}{4} \div \frac{7}{6}}$

(b) $3.5 \div \left(\dfrac{5.6}{1.4} - 1.9\right)$

26. Estimate the values of:

(a) $\dfrac{61.068 \times 0.049\,5}{0.987}$

(b) $\dfrac{4.899 + 7.265}{1.756}$

27. Estimate the values of:

(a) $\dfrac{51.98 + 29.87}{59.21 - 21.21}$

(b) $\dfrac{11.868 \times 3.001}{1.786}$

28. Estimate the values of the following, correct the answers to 1 significant figure.

(a) $\dfrac{1\,202}{61 \times 399}$

(b) $\dfrac{48.9 \times 802 \times 0.011}{4.98 \times 20.01}$

29. Estimate, to 1 significant figure, the values of:

(a) $\dfrac{4\,480}{28.99}$

(b) $\dfrac{39.5 \times 501.27}{102.11}$

(c) $4.89 \times 10.67 \times 5.76$

30. Estimate the value of the following to 2 significant figures.
$$\dfrac{6.29 \times 7.68}{9.112 \div 2.998}$$

31. Without using a calculator, estimate the following, correct the answers to 2 significant figures.

(a) $2\,995.78 \div 9.95$

(b) $\dfrac{589.25 \times 39.65}{79.63 \times 9.89}$

(c) $\dfrac{0.499\,5 \times 14.85 \times 69.978}{7.212 \times 19.775}$

5

Time : 1 hour

Marks : 50

*Answer all the questions **without** the use of a calculator.*

1. Evaluate:
   (a) $16 \div 0.5$ [1]
   (b) $(7.8 - 0.6) \times 7$ [1]

   Ans (a) _____

   (b) _____

2. Evaluate:
   (a) $8.95 + 12.7 + 0.63$ [1]

   (b) $\dfrac{1}{5} + \dfrac{2}{3}$ [1]

   Ans (a) _____

   (b) _____

3. (a) Express 5 326 correct to 2 significant figures. [1]

(b) Express $\dfrac{7}{60}$ as a decimal, correct to 3 decimal places. [1]

Ans (a) _____

(b) _____

4. Calculate the following:

(a) $3 \times 5.25 \div \left(0.7 - \dfrac{1}{4}\right)$ [4]

(b) $7.5 \div 3\dfrac{3}{4} \times \left(\dfrac{3}{5} + 2.25\right)$ [4]

Ans (a) _____

(b) _____

7

5. For each of the following, arrange the fractions and/or decimals in ascending order.

(a) $\frac{2}{3}, \frac{2}{5}, 0.45, 0.95$ [2]

(b) $\frac{3}{5}, \frac{3}{7}, 0.3, 0.5$ [2]

(c) $\frac{4}{9}, \frac{7}{13}, \frac{9}{20}, \frac{3}{8}$ [2]

(d) $0.2\dot{4}, \frac{1}{5}, 0.2\dot{4}\dot{5}, 0.25$ [2]

Ans (a) _____

(b) _____

(c) _____

(d) _____

6. Find the HCF and LCM of the following sets of numbers.
   (a) 36, 450, 108 [4]
   (b) 700, 35, 315 [4]
   (c) 26, 65, 130 [4]
   (d) 121, 231, 154 [4]

Ans (a) _____

(b) _____

(c) _____

(d) _____

7. Estimate, correct to 1 significant figure, the value of:

(a) $\dfrac{9.01 \times 24.01}{2.999}$ [2]

(b) $53.945\,812 - 27.342\,861$ [2]

Ans (a) _____

(b) _____

8. Find the exact value of the following:

(a) $1\frac{1}{3} \times 2\frac{1}{2} \div 1\frac{1}{2}$ [2]

(b) $\dfrac{4 - \dfrac{3}{5}}{4 + \dfrac{3}{5}}$ [2]

(c) $\left(5\frac{1}{3} \times \frac{1}{4}\right) - \left(2\frac{1}{3} \div 3\frac{1}{2}\right)$ [2]

(d) 0.3×0.45 [2]

Ans (a) _____

(b) _____

(c) _____

(d) _____

Arithmetic Problems

1. Express
   - **(a)** 10.03 g in kg,
   - **(b)** 1 010 g in kg and g,
   - **(c)** 100 kg 1 g in g,
   - **(d)** 7.4 km in m,
   - **(e)** 1.01 m in cm,
   - **(f)** 3.2 cm in m,
   - **(g)** 601 cm in m and cm,
   - **(h)** 13 min in s,
   - **(i)** 2 h 23 min in min,
   - **(j)** 301 s in min and s,
   - **(k)** 2 h 15 min 20 s in s.

2. Find the number of minutes between 21 20 and 23 37.

3. Express 817 mm in cm, giving your answer correct to the nearest cm.

4. Find the cost of 29 bags which costs $17.95 each.

5. How much does 63.156 litres of petrol cost if the price of 2 litres of petrol is $2.13?

6. Calculate the total time 7 buses take to get to town A if each of them took 2 h 35 min.

7. Calculate the total cost of 6 articles priced at $2.27 each and 3 articles priced at $3.84 each.

8. Calculate the total cost of $3\frac{1}{2}$ metres of ribbon at 60 cents per metre and 30 buttons at 7 cents each.

9. Calculate the total cost of the following shopping bill.

Rice	$4.80
Mushrooms	$1.05
Prawns	$6.50
Noodles	$0.95

10. A man bought a cake and immediately ate $\frac{1}{8}$ of it. Six hours later, he ate $\frac{2}{5}$ of the remaining cake and gave $\frac{1}{4}$ of the uneaten cake to his dog. What fraction of the cake was left?

11. Each week a family spends $\frac{5}{16}$ of its income on food, $\frac{1}{4}$ on housing, $\frac{1}{24}$ on clothes and $\frac{1}{48}$ on transport. If there is $27 left, calculate the weekly income.

12. Two-fifths of the students in a school stay to have lunch in school. There are 890 students altogether. How many students do not have lunch in school?

13. There are two bags of rice. One bag weighs $76\frac{5}{6}$ kg and the other weighs $42\frac{2}{3}$ kg. If $\frac{5}{7}$ of the total weight is sold, find the weight of the remaining rice.

14. A pen costs 45 cents and a book costs $2.65. Calculate the cost of
    (a) 4 pens and 2 books,
    (b) 5 pens and 3 books.

15. The product of two fractions is $\frac{5}{8}$. One of the fractions is $2\frac{11}{32}$. Find the other fraction.

16. If a bag costs $3.99, how much do 17 such bags cost? How many bags can I buy with $91.77?

17. Susan spends $4.75 on some packets of chocolates.
    (a) How much change can she get if she uses $10 to pay for her purchase?
    (b) Each packet of chocolates costs 95 cents. How many packets of chocolates has Susan bought?

18. (a) How many minutes are there in $3\frac{1}{2}$ hours?
    (b) Find the number of minutes between 08 35 and 10 18.
    (c) An examination lasts $2\frac{1}{2}$ hours. It starts at 14 50. At what time will it end?

19. There are 252 marbles in a bag. If $\frac{2}{7}$ of them are red, $\frac{4}{9}$ of the remainder are green and the rest are blue, how many blue marbles are there?

20. A car can travel $17\frac{1}{2}$ km on 2 litres of petrol. If 1 litre of petrol costs $1.42, find how much it costs to travel a distance of $87\frac{1}{2}$ km.

21. A piece of string was $7\frac{4}{9}$ m long. A boy cut off $1\frac{5}{18}$ m of the string and gave it to his sister. He then cut off $\frac{2}{3}$ of the remaining length for his cousin. What was the length of the remaining piece of string?

22. Two police cars, P and Q, from a police station patrol a housing estate every night. Car P takes 25 min to cover a route, while car Q takes 40 min to cover a different route. If both of them start at midnight, at what time will they meet at the police station again?

23. Two bells toll together at 10 45. One bell tolls every 9 min and the other every 12 min. When will they next toll together?

24. (a) The height of four boys are 1.45 m, 1.31 m, 1.21 m and 1.42 m. Find their average height.

(b) The average weight of four girls, whose weights are 36 kg, 50 kg, 40 kg and x kg, is 41 kg. Find the value of x.

25. A number is multiplied by 3 and added to 5. The result is the same as subtracting 9 from the number. Find the number.

26. The following shows the price list of some items:

Condensed milk	90¢
Corned beef	$2.95
Soybean oil	$5.50
Sliced ham (per 100 g)	96¢

Calculate how much Mrs Yong needs to pay if she buys 2 tins of condensed milk, 2 tins of corned beef, 3 bottles of soybean oil and 300 g of sliced ham.

27. Ali and Jimmy work for a delivery company as part-time delivery boys. They are paid the same amount for each day they worked. Ali works for 3 days and Jimmy works for the remaining 4 days of the week. Jimmy earns $97.20 every week. How much does Ali earn for every week?

28. On a tour, the total of all the children's fares is $96. Given that the fare for one child is $6 and that a child's fare is $\frac{4}{5}$ that of an adult's, calculate

(a) the number of children on the tour,

(b) the adult fare.

29. (a) Add together the following, giving your answer in hours and minutes.
$$35 \text{ min} + 2 \text{ h } 15 \text{ min} + 5 \text{ h } 48 \text{ min}$$

(b) Mary takes 23 minutes to walk to school. She does this 5 times a week. How many hours and minutes does Mary take altogether to walk to school each week?

30. A shopkeeper ordered 30 dozen eggs from a wholesaler, who charged him 95 cents for every dozen. When his order arrived, he discovered that 20 of the eggs were broken. He kept 30 eggs for his family and sold the rest. Calculate how much profit he made if he charged his customers 15 cents for an egg.

31. Mr Zheng visits the pet shop every four days to buy seeds for his birds. Mr Chen visits the same shop every six days to buy tubifex worms for his fish. If both of them visit the shop on the first day of the month, when will they visit the shop again on the same day?

32. (a) A woman owed the bank $536.65. She then paid into her account a cheque for $700.20. Find the amount of money she had altogether in her account, correct to the nearest dollar.

(b) Multiply 78.5 by 0.021 and then subtract the result from 19.

33. A man uses his car only 4 days a week. His car uses 3 litres, 8 litres, 5 litres and 6 litres of petrol on each day respectively.
    (a) Find the average amount of petrol he uses in a week.
    (b) If petrol costs 138 cents per litre, calculate the amount of money he spends on petrol in a week.

34. Three boys, A, B and C, share the use of a computer for one day as shown in the following table.

	A	B	C
Number of times	3	1	5
Time spent/min	90	125	89

    (a) Calculate, in hours and minutes, the time spent by A and C respectively on the computer in a day.
    (b) Calculate the average time spent on the computer by the boys in a day.

35. The table below shows the amount of pocket money students in a class receive weekly.

Number of students	Amount of money each student receives
6	$2.00
15	$3.00
7	$4.00
3	$5.00
3	$10.00

    (a) Find the number of students in the class.
    (b) Find the total amount of money the students receive each week.

36. A car owner noted down the distance he travelled for the first six months of a year in the following table.

Month	Distance travelled/km
January	840
February	1 000
March	3 500
April	2 500
May	800
June	2 880

    (a) What was the average monthly distance travelled?
    (b) What was the amount he spent on petrol for half a year if the cost of petrol was $40.50 for every 32 km travelled?

37. The following table shows the number of plates two dishwashers can wash in a given time.

	Number of plates	Time taken/min
Dishwasher 1	10	6
Dishwasher 2	20	8

How many plates can both dishwashers wash in 1 h?

38. A girl receives a weekly wage of $75 for working a 25-hour week.
  (a) Calculate her hourly rate of pay.
  (b) If she works overtime, she is paid twice the amount she normally receives for one hour of work. Find the amount she is paid for one hour of overtime.
  (c) Calculate the amount she will earn in a week if she works 43 h.
  (d) At the beginning of the year, the girl opens a bank account. Each month, she deposits $30.25 into her account. After six months, her account is credited with $18.05 of interest. At the end of the year, her account is credited with a further $40.50 of interest. Calculate the amount of money she has in her bank account at the end of the year.

39. Amy is paid $2.50 an hour for the first 50 h she works each week. If she works overtime, she is paid an additional $\frac{3}{5}$ of this amount for an hour.
  (a) How much does she earn for one hour of overtime?
  (b) If she works 57 h in one week, how much does she earn?
  (c) If she earns $193 in one week, how many hours has she worked?

40. A company hires out small and large minibuses. A small minibus can be hired for $35 per day and a large minibus can be hired for $50 per day. If the total distance travelled during the total period of hire is 200 km or less, no extra charge is required. However, every kilometre travelled over 200 km is charged at 8¢ per extra kilometre for the small minibus and 12¢ per extra kilometre for the large minibus.
  (a) A small minibus was hired for 2 days and travelled 220 km during the period of hire. Calculate the total hire charge.
  (b) A man who hired a large minibus for 3 days was charged $156.72. Calculate the total distance he travelled.

16

41. A firm rents out campervans and cars at $45 and $55 per day respectively. The table below shows the charges for the distance travelled during the period of hire.

Type of vehicles	Distance travelled	Charges for each kilometre over 280 km
Cars and campervans	⩽ 280 km	no extra charge
Campervans	> 280 km	9¢ per extra km
Cars	> 280 km	11¢ per extra km

   (a) Calculate the total charge of a campervan that was hired for 4 days and travelled 320 km during the period of hire.

   (b) A man paid $169.95 for hiring a car for 3 days. Calculate the total distance he travelled during the 3 days.

42. A woman went on a shopping spree and bought the following items shown in the table.

Item	Number of each item	Price of each item
Blouse	6	$59.90 each
Shoes	7	$49.00 each
Stockings	18	$1.95 each

   (a) Calculate, in dollars and cents, the total amount of money spent.

   (b) If the woman was a buyer of a department store, and she ordered 580 more of the same blouse (at $59.90 each) and 210 more pairs of the same shoes (at $49.00 each), but no stockings, estimate the amount she spent to the nearest dollar.

43. I use an average of 802.9 units of electricity per month.

   (a) Estimate, to the nearest dollar, the total amount of the bill, if one unit of electricity costs 8.6 cents together with a surcharge of $28.50 which I have to pay.

   (b) In one year, the cost per unit of electricity increased from 8.6 cents to 9.8 cents, while the surcharge remained unchanged. Estimate, to the nearest dollar, the total amount of the whole year's electricity bills if I continue to use an average of 802.9 units of electricity per month.

17

1. Evaluate $[-3 + (-15)] + (-7 + 56)$.

2. Evaluate $(-15) - (-80) + (-31)$.

3. Complete the following number patterns.
   (a) 3, 6, 9, 12, _____ , _____ , _____ , _____
   (b) −4, _____ , 0, 2, _____ , _____ , _____
   (c) −15, _____ , _____ , 0, _____ , 10, _____

4. Calculate the following:
   (a) $367 - 520$ (b) $-498 - (-382)$
   (c) $144 - 398 - 105$ (d) $213 - 766 + 438$
   (e) $614 - (-133) + (-220)$ (f) $-747 - (-123) - (-246)$

5. Calculate the following:
   (a) -53×17 (b) $29 \times (-13)$
   (c) $-97 \times (-18)$ (d) $0 \times (-36)$

6. Find the products of the following:
   (a) $-8 \times (-3) \times 2$ (b) $-10 \times (-4) \times (-5) \times (-2)$
   (c) $-12 \times 8 \times (-14)$ (d) $15 \times (-5) \times (-3)$

7. Given that $\sqrt{4.25} = 2.062$ and $\sqrt{42.5} = 6.519$, evaluate:
   (a) $\sqrt{425}$ (b) $\sqrt{4\,250}$

8. Use your calculator to complete the following, giving your answers correct to 3 decimal places.
   $$(5.29)^2 - (2.36)^2 =$$

9. Evaluate $\sqrt{0.25}$ correct to the nearest whole number.

10. By expressing 78 400 as 784×100, find, without using the calculator, the square root of 78 400.

11. Find the value of a if $\sqrt{a} = \sqrt{1\,225} - \sqrt{576}$.

12. Find the cube root of each of the following numbers.
    (a) −2 197   (b) 9 261
    (c) 729   (d) −3 375

18

13. (a) Express 3 136 as a product of prime factors.

(b) Hence find the square root of 3 136.

14. Evaluate the following:

(a) $-56 \div (-7)$ (b) $-720 \div (9)$

(c) $232 \div (-8)$ (d) $-1\,083 \div (-19) \div (-3)$

(e) $1\,575 \div [-(-15)] \div [-(-7)]$

15. Find the square roots of:

(a) $\dfrac{16}{25}$ (b) 0.81 (c) $7\dfrac{1}{9}$

16. Evaluate:

(a) $1\dfrac{9}{10} - 2\dfrac{4}{5}\left[1\dfrac{3}{5}\left(\dfrac{2}{7} + \dfrac{3}{4} - \dfrac{9}{14}\right)\right]$

(b) $1\dfrac{1}{3} - 3\dfrac{1}{2} - \left(-\dfrac{4}{3}\right) + \left(-2\dfrac{1}{4}\right)$

17. (a) Evaluate $\sqrt{1\dfrac{11}{25}}$.

(b) Using as much of the information below as is necessary, evaluate $\sqrt{4\,720}$.

$[\sqrt{4.72} = 2.173,\ \sqrt{47.2} = 6.870]$

18. Evaluate the following, giving your answer as a single fraction in its simplest form.

(a) $4\dfrac{1}{3} - 2\dfrac{5}{7}$ (b) $\dfrac{5}{16} \div \left(2\dfrac{1}{2}\right)^2$

19. Find

(a) the square of 3^{-2},

(b) the square root of $3^0 + 3^1 + 3^2 + 3^3 + 3^4$,

(c) the reciprocal of $2^1 + 2^2$,

(d) the cube of $\dfrac{2^3 \times 3^2}{6^3}$,

(e) the cube root of $3^4 - 2^4 - 1^4$.

20. Evaluate

(a) $\sqrt{5\,184} \div \sqrt{2\,025}$,   (b) $\dfrac{\sqrt{1\,764} - \sqrt{784}}{(7 + 9)^2}$

Express your answers as fractions.

21. Evaluate $\dfrac{(1.2)^2 - (0.5)^2}{(2.5)^2 - (1.5)^2}$.

22. Evaluate $\sqrt{441} - \dfrac{1}{\sqrt{576}}$.

23. Evaluate:

    (a) $\sqrt{2\,304}$ **(b)** $\sqrt{1\dfrac{24}{25}} + \sqrt{1\dfrac{7}{9}}$ **(c)** $\sqrt{0.000\,625}$

24. Using a calculator, evaluate the following and round off the answers correct to 3 significant figures.

    (a) $-\dfrac{1.44}{6} - 6.895$ **(b)** $\dfrac{(1.5)^2 - (2.5)^2}{(0.5)^2}$

25. Use a calculator to evaluate the following correct to 3 significant figures.

$$\frac{\sqrt{8.9} - \sqrt{2.1}}{(5.2)^2 + (7.6)^2}$$

26. Evaluate:

    (a) $\sqrt{400}$ **(b)** $\sqrt{\dfrac{25}{9}} - \sqrt{\dfrac{81}{36}}$

27. Evaluate $7 \div [(-2 - 5) \times (15 - 8)] + (-6 + 4) \div (16 - 20)$.

28. Evaluate:
    (a) $-14 + 2 \times [(-18 - 10) \times -7 + 3]$
    (b) $93 + 42 - [12 + (-5)] \times 5$

29. Evaluate $15^2 + 7^2 \times 3$.

30. Evaluate:
    (a) $5^2 \times 7^2 - 50$ **(b)** $(50^2 - 8^2 \times 6^2) \div 4$

31. Evaluate:
    (a) $[5.3 + (-7.5)] - (-1.4 - 2.6) \times (-0.5)$
    (b) $(3 + 5)^2 - (17 - 5)^2 \div 2\dfrac{2}{5}$

32. Evaluate $[-3 + (-15)] + (-7 + 56)$.

33. Evaluate:
    (a) $(-5 + 17) \times [-38 - 3 \times (-7)] - 2 \times (-4)$
    (b) $[5.3 - (-2.9)] \div (-5.65 + 4.21)$

34. Evaluate $-\dfrac{3}{2}\left[\left(\dfrac{8}{3} - \dfrac{1}{2}\right) \times \left(6\dfrac{1}{2}\right)\right]$.

35. Evaluate $(\sqrt{2.25} - \sqrt{4.84}) + (-8) \div (-2)$.

36. Evaluate:

    (a) $-0.08 \times (5.28 - 9.54)$ **(b)** $\dfrac{(2.5)^2 \times 5}{(1.5)^2}$

37. Evaluate $-\left[\left(2\dfrac{2}{5} - 4\right) \div \dfrac{16}{5}\right] + 8\dfrac{1}{2}$.

38. Evaluate $\sqrt{1\dfrac{9}{16} + \dfrac{9}{5} \div 1\dfrac{1}{5}}$.

39. Without using a calculator, evaluate:

    (a) $7\dfrac{1}{3} \div 1\dfrac{2}{9} - \dfrac{5}{8}$ **(b)** $(0.2)^3 - (1.3)^2$

40. Evaluate:
    (a) $42 - 48 \div (-4) - 101$ **(b)** $(6 + 2) \times (-2) + (-8)$

41. Evaluate:

    (a) $5\dfrac{1}{4} \times \left(1\dfrac{5}{7}\right)^2$

    (b) $7.8 - 3.2 \times 0.05$

42. Estimate the value of $(\sqrt{3.98} - \sqrt{16.125}) \div 6.08$.

43. Evaluate:
    (a) $[-7 + (7 - 2.5) \div (-6)] \times 3$ **(b)** $[-8 + (-6) \times 4] \div (-2 - 6)$

44. **(a)** Evaluate $3.7^2 + 3.7 \times 0.3$.
    (b) Find the number which when divided by 0.023 gives an exact value of 1.8.

TEST PAPER 2

Time : 1 hour

Marks : 50

1. (a) Given that 1 cm^3 of ice has a mass of 8.3×10^{-1} g, find, in grams, the mass of 500 cm^3 of ice. [2]

   (b) Convert 36 metres per second to kilometres per hour. [2]

   Ans (a) _____

   (b) _____

2. Write down the positive square root of each of the following:

   (a) 8 100 [2]

   (b) $7\dfrac{1}{9}$ [2]

   Ans (a) _____

   (b) _____

3. Using as much of the information given below as is necessary, write down the value of $\sqrt{0.023}$. [$\sqrt{23} = 4.796$, $\sqrt{2.3} = 1.517$] [2]

Ans _____'

4. Evaluate the following:

(a) $\sqrt{\dfrac{5}{6} \times \dfrac{3}{2} \div \dfrac{5}{8}}$ [4]

(b) $-\dfrac{1}{6} + \left[\left(-\dfrac{2}{3}\right) + \dfrac{1}{3}\right] \div \left(-\dfrac{1}{5}\right)$ [4]

(c) $-\left(\dfrac{5}{19}\right) + \left(\dfrac{-13}{-38}\right) - \left(\dfrac{4}{15} \times \dfrac{45}{-12} \times 2\right)$ [4]

Ans (a) _____

(b) _____

(c) _____

5. The average mark of five boys was 58 and a sixth boy scored 46. What was the average mark of the six boys? [4]

Ans _____

6. A soya bean drink cost 45¢.
   (a) Find the cost of 5 soya bean drinks. [3]
   (b) If you had $5.00, how many drinks would you be able to buy? [3]

Ans (a) _____

(b) _____

7. Mr Ng works $7\frac{1}{2}$ hours each night. He starts work at 23 15 and earns $67.50 each night.

   (a) At what time does he finish work? [2]

   (b) How much does he earn in one hour? [2]

   (c) For working 5 nights per week, he earns an extra allowance of $30.00 per week. How much does he earn altogether if he works for 5 nights in one week? [5]

Ans (a) _____

(b) _____

(c) _____

8. **(a)** A reel contains 93.8 m of cotton. Calculate

      (i) the number of pieces of cotton, each of length 2.0 m, which can be cut from the reel, [2]

      (ii) the length, in centimetres, of the piece then remaining. [3]

   (b) A bank manager takes home a salary of $5 000 per month. He spends $\frac{2}{5}$ of his salary on his family, $\frac{3}{8}$ of the remainder on himself and saves the rest. How much can he save in 6 months? [4]

Ans (a) (i) _____

(ii) _____

(b) _____

26

CHAPTER 5

Simple Algebraic Expressions

1. Write an expression for each of the following:
   (a) The number which is 10 greater than the number m.
   (b) The number which is twice of n.
   (c) The number which is 5 less than the product of p and q.

2. The product of two numbers is 50. If one of the numbers is a, write an expression for the other.

3. Write down an expression for the cost, in dollars, of 30 pencils at x cents each and 16 pens at y cents each.

4. Jason, Peter and James have 45 marbles altogether. If Jason has w marbles and Peter has x marbles, how many marbles has James?

5. Meiling buys x apples and some oranges. She buys 3 more oranges than apples.
   (a) Write down, in terms of x, an expression for the number of oranges that Meiling buys.
   (b) Each apple costs 40¢ and each orange costs 50¢. Find, as simply as possible in terms of x, an expression for the total cost of the fruit that Meiling buys.

6. In the diagram, $ABCD$ is a trapezium in which AD is parallel to BC and $A\hat{B}C = 90°$. The side $AD = (x + 3)$ cm, $AB = (2x - 1)$ cm and $BC = (3x + 4)$ cm.

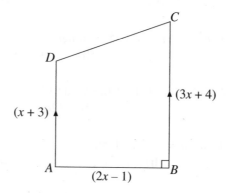

Write down, in terms of x, an expression for the area of the trapezium.

7. Five children took some cookies to a party. Alice took h cookies each of mass 20 g. Elizabeth took k cookies each of mass 15 g. Peter and David each took p cookies each of mass 25 g.
Write down an expression, in terms of h, k and p, for
   (a) the total number of cookies taken to the party,
   (b) the total mass of the cookies.

8. Peter has h dollars, John has k dollars and Joseph has 3 times of what Peter and John have. If they combine their money to buy a toy, they will get back a change of $2.00. Write an expression for the price of the toy.

9. If $a = 4\frac{1}{3}$, $b = 3\frac{2}{5}$, $c = 5\frac{1}{2}$ and $d = 3$, evaluate
   (a) $\dfrac{ab}{d}$,
   (b) $\dfrac{c + b}{c - d}$.

10. If $a = 3$, $b = -2$ and $c = -3$, evaluate
   (a) $\dfrac{a - b}{ab}$,
   (b) $a(b - c)$.

11. Given that $x = 5$ and $y = -3$, find the value of
   (a) $y^2 + xy$,
   (b) $(2x - y)(x - 2y)$.

12. Given that $\dfrac{2p + 3q}{q} = \dfrac{3}{8}$, find the value of $\dfrac{p}{q}$.

13. Given that $a = -3$ and $b = 6$, find the value of
   (a) $-5a + b$,
   (b) $8a^3 - b$.

14. Given that $x = 5$, $y = 3$ and $z = -2$, evaluate
   (a) $2x^2 - y$,
   (b) $y(x - z)$.

15. Given that $p = 3$, $q = -5$ and $r = -2$, evaluate
   (a) $2p^2$,
   (b) $p - r^2$,
   (c) $p(r - q)$.

16. Given that $a = 3$, $b = -2$ and $c = 5$, evaluate
   (a) $a^2 + b^2$,
   (b) $(a + 2c)(b + 2c)$.

17. Given that $a = 4$ and $b = -3$, find the value of
   (a) ab^2,
   (b) $(2a + b)^3$.

18. Given that $p = 4$ and $q = -2$, evaluate
   (a) $2p + 5q$,
   (b) $7 - q^2$,
   (c) $q(p - q)$.

19. Evaluate $\dfrac{x - y}{x + y}$ when $x = 5$ and $y = -3$.

28

20. Given that $h = 7$ and $k = -1$, evaluate
    (a) $3h + 4k$,   **(b)** $2h^2$,   **(c)** $h(3k - 10)$.

21. Given that $a = -4$, $b = 3$ and $c = 0$, find the value of
    (a) abc,   **(b)** $a - 2b + 3c$,
    (c) $a^2 - b^2 + c^2$.

22. Evaluate the following by taking $p = 4$, $q = \dfrac{1}{2}$, $r = -3$ and $s = -\dfrac{3}{4}$.

    (a) $5p + (r - s)$ **(b)** $\dfrac{1}{2}(2p - 3q) + \dfrac{r}{s}$

    (c) $7pr^2 + 4q^2s$ **(d)** $rs\left(\dfrac{1}{p} - \dfrac{1}{q}\right)$

    (e) $3p^2q - 6sr$ **(f)** $pr + r[(q + 8s - pq) - 6q]$

23. Find the product of the following:
    (a) $7w$ and $5x$ **(b)** $3w$ and $-8x$ **(c)** $6m$ and $7n^2$
    (d) $9pq$ and $-4p^2q$ **(e)** $15c$ and $-9c$ **(f)** $-4a$ and $-23a$

24. Find the quotient
    (a) when $168a^2$ is divided by $12a$,
    (b) when $-49xy$ is divided by $-14y$,
    (c) when $44p$ is divided by $-66pq$,
    (d) when $52c(-d)$ is divided by $4b(-c)$,
    (e) when $-17rs$ is divided by $85p(-r)$,
    (f) when $24ab$ is divided by $\dfrac{1}{3}ab^2$.

25. Simplify:
    (a) $10a + b - 15a + 3b$ **(b)** $2(a + b) - 5(a + 2b)$
    (c) $\dfrac{1}{3}(2x + y) - \dfrac{5}{6}x + \dfrac{2}{9}y$

26. Simplify $5x - 4[2x - (6y - 3x)]$.

27. Simplify:

    (a) $4(a + 3b) - 15b$ **(b)** $\dfrac{1}{3}[4a - (6 - 5a)]$

28. Simplify $-5a - \dfrac{1}{3}a + 3\left(\dfrac{1}{6}a - 7\right)$.

29. Simplify:

    (a) $\dfrac{2x - 5}{3} - \dfrac{3x - 7}{5}$ **(b)** $\dfrac{1}{5}x - \dfrac{7}{2}\left[\dfrac{6}{21}x - \left(\dfrac{3}{7}y - \dfrac{1}{14}x\right)\right]$

30. Simplify $3x^2 - 4x + 3 + x^2 + 2x - 4$.

31. Simplify:
   (a) $7 - 4x - 8(x + 2)$
   (b) $5x - x^2 + 3x^2 - x + y$

32. Simplify:
   (a) $\dfrac{1}{3}\left(\dfrac{5}{2}a - \dfrac{7}{2}b\right) - \dfrac{2}{5}\left(\dfrac{3}{2}a - \dfrac{1}{3}b\right)$
   (b) $8[5a - (2a - 3c)]$

33. Simplify:
   (a) $4(3t - 2) - 3(t + 5)$
   (b) $\dfrac{x + 4}{5} + \dfrac{1 - x}{3}$

34. Simplify the following:
   (a) $5x - 3(y - x)$
   (b) $4(2t - 3) - 2(5t + 2)$
   (c) $5(2y - 3) - 2(7 - 3y)$
   (d) $(a + 3b) - (-2b + 5a)$
   (e) $15(1 - 3p) + 3(p^2 - 2p)$
   (f) $(-x - y) - (-y - 2x)$
   (g) $2a + (-3b + 4a)$

35. Simplify the following expressions:
   (a) $15a^2 - (-7a) + 14a^2 - 6a$
   (b) $12p - q + 6p + 25q + 13r - p^2$
   (c) $4w^2 + 5p^2 - (-3w^2) - (-7p^2) + 10w$
   (d) $a(3b + 4c) - 2c(5a - 2b)$
   (e) $h(j - 3k) - j(3h - 2k) - k(5h + 4j)$
   (f) $2w[x + y(x^2 - w) - 2] - 7wx + 4x^2yw - (-5w^2y)$

36. Simplify the following expressions:
   (a) $\dfrac{1}{3}(27a + 9) - 5$
   (b) $\dfrac{3}{4}(p + 1) - \dfrac{1}{8}(p - 3)$
   (c) $\dfrac{1}{7}(28x^2 - 5) - \dfrac{1}{21}(9 - 15x^2)$
   (d) $\dfrac{4x - 3}{15} + \dfrac{5x + 6}{20}$
   (e) $\dfrac{2(4p - q)}{8} - \dfrac{3p - 7q}{16}$
   (f) $\dfrac{w}{3} - \dfrac{2x}{5} + 4$

37. Simplify:
   (a) $2x - [5x - 7y - 8(9x - 2y)]$
   (b) $-6(3r - s) + 4(r - 5s)$

CHAPTER 6

Open Sentences and Equations

1. Solve the equation $4x - 9 = 15$.

2. Solve the equation $\dfrac{x}{4} - 5 = \dfrac{1}{5}(x - 20)$.

3. Solve the equation $\dfrac{x + 1}{4} + \dfrac{2x + 1}{3} = 1$.

4. Solve the equation $\dfrac{7}{5}x - 9 = \dfrac{1}{2}x$.

5. Solve the equation $x^2 - 2x - 36 = -2x$.

6. Solve the equation $\dfrac{9y}{16} = \dfrac{1}{9y}$.

7. Solve the equation $2x(x - 1) = 162 - 2x$.

8. Solve the equation $5(x - 1) + 2(2x - 1) = 11$.

9. Solve the equation $\dfrac{5}{2}x + 10 = \dfrac{5}{3}x$.

10. Solve the equation $2t = \dfrac{18}{t}$.

11. Solve the equation $3(1 - 4x) = 4(2x + 1)$.

12. Solve the equation $2x(x + 1) - (2x - 3) = 165$.

13. Solve the equation $5x - 3 = 2(x - 3) - 18$.

14. Solve the following equations:

    (a) $3x + 8 = -1$

    (b) $\dfrac{1}{4}x - 16 = 4$

    (c) $5x + 7 = 6 - 9x$

    (d) $3(2x + 3) - (5 - x) = 12 - 4x$

    (e) $7(u - 3) = 42$

    (f) $4(a - 5) - 3(1 - a) = 0$

15. Solve the following equations:

(a) $\dfrac{3x + 1}{4} = \dfrac{7x - 2}{5}$

(b) $\dfrac{x + 1}{2} - \dfrac{x + 3}{3} = 5$

(c) $\dfrac{3}{v} - 4 = 3$

(d) $\dfrac{2}{w} + \dfrac{3}{w} = \dfrac{1}{18}$

(e) $\dfrac{1}{a + 7} = \dfrac{1}{5}$

(f) $\dfrac{6}{5x} + 1 = \dfrac{3}{x}$

16. Solve the following equations:

(a) $8.2x - 4.5 = 3.3$

(b) $2.7 - 1.2x = 0.04$

(c) $2(1.5x - 1) = 5.7x + 3.8$

(d) $6.1(x + 3) = 2.3(3x - 5)$

(e) $5(2.2y - 4) = 10.7y$

(f) $9.4y - 3 = -6.3y - (-10)$

17. Given that $A = \sqrt{4x + y}$,

(a) find the value of A if $x = 60$ and $y = 16$,

(b) find the value of x if $A = 5$ and $y = -7$.

18. Given that $v^2 = u^2 + 2as$, find the value of v when $u = 10$, $a = 4$ and $s = 15$.

19. Given that $A = \dfrac{1}{2}(p + q)h$, find the value of A when $p = 12$, $q = 6$ and $h = 5$.

20. Given that $x = \sqrt{3y}$, find

(a) x when $y = 48$,

(b) y when $x = 48$.

21. Given that $F = \dfrac{9}{5}C + 32$, find the value of

(a) F when $C = 40$,

(b) C when $F = 250$.

22. The volume of a cone can be found by the formula $V = \dfrac{1}{3}\pi r^2 h$. Calculate the value of V if $r = 4$ cm, $h = 12.5$ cm and $\pi = \dfrac{22}{7}$.

23. Given that $p = \sqrt[3]{3q - r}$, find the value of p when $q = 3$ and $r = 7$.

24. It is given that $R = \dfrac{km^2}{n}$ and that $R = 24$ when $m = 2$ and $n = 3$. Calculate the value of k.

25. One quarter of a number added to 10 gives the same result as when $\dfrac{1}{3}$ of it is subtracted from 31. What is the number?

26. The sum of two consecutive even numbers is 66. Find the product of these two numbers.

27. Alan spends p cents of his pocket money every day. How much will he spend in 20 weeks?

28. A woman decides to give money to each of her three daughters on their birthdays. Shulin is to receive $3 000 more than Suyi. Suqing is to have 4 times as much as Suyi.
    (a) If Suyi receives $\$x$, then Shulin receives $\$(x + 3\ 000)$. Write an expression for the amount Suqing receives in terms of x.
    (b) Suppose Suqing receives $1 600, how much does Shulin receive?
    (c) If Suqing and Shulin receive the same amount of money, how much does their mother give altogether?

29. A boy spent $9.05 on pens and pencils. If one dozen pens cost $13.20 and he bought 7 pencils and 6 pens, find the cost of one dozen pencils.

30. A man used $3 to pay for 16 postage stamps. x of them are 15¢ each and the rest 20¢ each.
    (a) Write down an equation in terms of x and find the value of x.
    (b) Is the man supposed to receive any change? If so, find the amount.

31. A box contains 3 paperback books which cost an average of $9.70 and 6 hard-cover books which cost an average of $55. Calculate the average cost of the books in the box.

32. I am eight years younger than Alex. In 9 years' time, the sum of our ages will be 76. How old is Alex now?

33. An adult ticket to an exhibition cost $5 while a child's ticket cost $2. If the number of children going to the exhibition was 3 more than the number of adults and a total amount of $20 was spent on the tickets, find the number of adults going to the exhibition.

34.

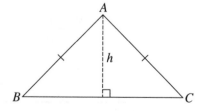

Given that ABC is an isosceles triangle, where $AB = AC$, $AB = (2x - 3)$ cm, $BC = (4x - 1)$ cm and the perimeter of the triangle is 110 cm, find
    (a) the value of x,
    (b) the area of the triangle if the height, h, is 10 cm.

35. The sum of two consecutive odd numbers is 44. Find the numbers.

36. A school has a field in the shape as shown below:

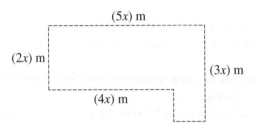

(5x) m

(2x) m

(3x) m

(4x) m

Calculate the value of x in each of the following cases:
(a) The perimeter of the field is 288 metres.
(b) The cost of fencing the field at $2.50 per metre is $3 200.

37. Mr Lim buys x crates of fruit for a total of $150 and intends to sell them at a profit of 50 cents per crate. Write down, in terms of x, expressions for
(a) the price, in dollars, that Mr Lim pays for one crate,
(b) his intended selling price, in dollars, of one crate.
When he has sold all the fruit, he finds that he has received $175. Find the number of crates he bought.

38. Mrs Tan spends $18.50 in buying 100 postage stamps. If x of them are 20¢ stamps and the remaining are 15¢ stamps. Find the number of the respective stamps that she bought.

39. Mr Yong purchased a number of books at $3.50 each and twice as many books at $9.50 each. The total cost came to $135. If x is the number of $3.50 books purchased, write down an equation in x and solve it. Hence find the total number of books purchased.

40.

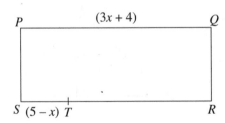

P   (3x + 4)   Q

S (5 – x) T   R

In the above diagram, *PQRS* is a rectangle and *T* is a point on *SR*. $PQ = (3x + 4)$ cm, $ST = (5 - x)$ cm and the perimeter of the rectangle is $(8x + 2)$ cm. Giving each answer in its simplest form, find in terms of x, an expression for
(a) *TR*,   **(b)** *PS*.

41. **(a)** In 1996, petrol cost $1.20 per litre. Calculate the number of litres of petrol that could be bought for $48.00.

(b) In 1997, the price of petrol was increased by x cents per litre. Write down an expression, in terms of x, for

  (i) the cost of one litre of petrol in 1997,

  (ii) the number of litres that could be bought for $36.00 in 1997.

(c) In 1998, the price was increased by a further x cents per litre. The quantity of petrol that cost $36.00 in 1997 now costs $38.25. Form an equation in x and solve it.

42. Meiling was paid $\$M$ per week. Her pay is made up of a basic wage of $80 plus 15 cents for each of the n customers she serves. The formula connecting M and n in this case is

$$M = 80 + \frac{15n}{100}$$

(a) Calculate the pay she received in a week when she served 360 customers.

(b) At the end of another week, Meiling received $140. How many customers did she serve?

(c) The employer decides to decrease Meiling's basic wage to $65 but to increase the pay per customer served to 21 cents. Write down the new formula connecting M and n.

(d) Find the number of customers Meiling would have to serve in a week for her to receive the same amount of money whichever formula is used.

1. Evaluate the following by taking $w = 7$, $x = \dfrac{2}{3}$, $y = -4$ and $z = -\dfrac{1}{5}$.

   (a) $\left[\dfrac{3x - y}{w - z}\right]^2$ [4]

   (b) $\left[\dfrac{1}{y^2} - 4w\right](x + z)$ [4]

   Ans (a) _____

   (b) _____

2. Simplify the following expressions:

   (a) $\dfrac{1}{6}(x - 1) + \dfrac{3}{4}(x + 5)$ [4]

   (b) $\dfrac{3(7y + 2)}{5} - \dfrac{7(4 - 2y)}{10}$ [4]

   Ans (a) _____

   (b) _____

3. Solve the following equations:

(a) $8(3 - 5x) - 7(1 - 4x) = -7$ [4]

(b) $5.8y - (-2.4) = 3(0.5 - 3.3y)$ [4]

(c) $\dfrac{2}{x + 5} = \dfrac{-3}{x}$ [4]

(d) $\dfrac{-1}{2y + 3} = 4$ [4]

Ans (a) _____

(b) _____

(c) _____

(d) _____

37

4. Given that $s = ut + \dfrac{1}{2}at^2$, find the value of

    (a) s when $a = 10$, $t = 3$ and $u = 5$,   [4]

    (b) u when $a = 8$, $s = 88$ and $t = 4$.   [4]

Ans (a) _____

(b) _____

5. The product of two numbers is 108. If one third of one of the numbers is 9, what are the numbers?   [4]

Ans _____ , _____

6. **(a)** A farmer has x tomato plants. He estimates that each plant will produce 4.5 kg of tomatoes. Write an expression, in terms of x, for the total mass of tomatoes that he expects to be produced. [1]

(b) He intends to apply 250 ml of liquid fertiliser to each plant. The fertiliser is sold in containers each holding 50 litres and costing $135 each. Write down an expression, in terms of x, for the number of containers of fertiliser he must buy. [2]

(c) If the total cost of the fertiliser is $810, form an equation in x and solve it.
[1 000 ml = 1 litre] [3]

Ans (a) _____

(b) _____

(c) _____

CHAPTER 7

Rate, Ratio and Percentage

1. Jason cycles 14.5 km in 50 min. Express his speed in km/h.

2. A man jogged 3.5 km in 20 min. He then walked the remainder of the 5.5 km at an average speed of 5 km/h. Given that he did not stop to rest during the entire distance of 5.5 km, calculate his average speed in km/h for the whole journey.

3. A man is driving at a speed of 60 km/h. Calculate the distance he will have travelled in 2 h and 15 min.

4. (a) A marathon race started at 09 30. One of the runners finished the race at 13 14. Calculate the time the runner took to run the race.
   (b) If the race was 78 km long, calculate the speed of a runner who took 4 h and 30 min to finish the race.

5. A man travelled for 90 min from town A to town B at an average speed of 18 km/h. He then travelled 6 km from town B to town C in 45 min.
   (a) Find the distance he travelled from town A to town B.
   (b) Find his average speed from town B to town C.
   (c) Find his average speed from town A to town C.

6. A boy cycled for 2 h at a certain speed and walked for another 2 h at a speed 4 km/h less than the cycling speed. Altogether, he travelled 36 km. At what speed did he walk?

7. A school bus takes 25 min to bring Xiaowen from her home to school, which is about 12 km away. What is the average speed of the bus in km/h?

8. A boy leaves his school at 13 38 and takes 90 min to travel home, which is 49.5 km away. Calculate
   (a) the time he reaches home,
   (b) his average speed in kilometres per hour.

9. (a) A red car is travelling from town A to town B which are 100 km apart. If the car travels at 60 km/h for the first 30 km and at 50 km/h for the rest of the journey, find the total time the car takes to get to town B.
   (b) Another car is also travelling from town A to town B. It is travelling at a constant speed of 80 km/h. Calculate, in hours and minutes, the difference in the arrival times of the two cars.

10. A man travels from A to B by coach at 70 km/h and then flies from B to A at 250 km/h. The total journey takes 15 hours.

(a) Find the distance from A to B in kilometres, correct the answer to 2 decimal places.

(b) Find the distance, in centimetres, which represents this distance from A to B on a map of scale 1 : 2 000 000.

11. A man left home and travelled 60 km for $5\frac{1}{2}$ h.

(a) If he set off from home at 11 45, find the time at which he reached his destination.

(b) Find his average speed for the whole journey.

12. Huihui walked for 35 min at a rate of 6 km/h, and then ran at a speed of $7\frac{1}{2}$ km/h for a certain period. At the end of that time, she was 10 km away from the starting point. Find the amount of time she spent on running.

13. Simplify the following ratios in their lowest terms.

(a) 72 : 432

(b) $\frac{5}{6} : \frac{1}{2}$

(c) 90 m to 6 m 90 cm

(d) 40 cm² to 1 m²

14. **(a)** If 5 : 9 = x : 63, find x.

(b) Given that y : 12 = 15 : 24, find y.

(c) If $2\frac{1}{4} : 3 = z : 1\frac{1}{5}$, find z.

15.

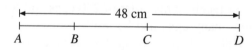

The line AD is 48 cm long. If $AB : BC : CD = 3 : 4 : 5$, calculate the length of BC.

16.

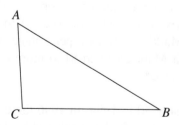

The lengths of the sides of triangle ABC are such that $AB : BC : CA = 6 : 5 : 3$. If AB = 9 cm, calculate the perimeter of triangle ABC.

17. **(a)** A man earning $12.50 a day receives an increase in the ratio 7 : 5. What is his new wage per week?

(b) In a camp, there is sufficient food to feed 140 campers for 16 meals. How many meals can the campers have if there are 224 of them?

18. A sum of money is divided among three people in the ratio 14 : 16 : 15. Given that the smallest share is $525, find the largest share.

19. $3 000 is shared among 4 people in the ratio 2 : 5 : 3 : 2.
(a) Calculate the smallest share.
(b) Calculate the largest share.

20. The perimeter of a rectangle is 28 cm. If the ratio of the length and breadth is 4 : 3, find
(a) the dimensions of the rectangle,
(b) the area of the rectangle.

21.

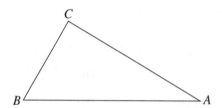

If the ratio of the size of $\hat{A}$, $\hat{B}$ and $\hat{C}$ is 1 : 2 : 3, find the size of $\hat{B}$.

22. $1 600 is shared among three people A, B and C in the ratio 1 : 2 : 5. Find the amount each will get.

23. **(a)** A shopkeeper received his order of 250 eggs and found that 8% of them were broken. How many eggs had he left?
(b) A sum of $480 is shared among three people in the ratio 3 : 5 : 8. Calculate the largest share.

24. **(a)** The postal charge for a certain parcel is increased from 60¢ to 80¢. Express the increase as a percentage of the original charge.
(b) A sum of money was divided between David and Mark in the ratio 1 : 4.
(i) Express Mark's share as a percentage of the total sum.
(ii) Given that Mark received $120 more than David, calculate the amount David received.

25. An antique clock cost $550 in 1994. In 1996 there was a 25% price increase. From 1996 to 1998, the price was further increased by 15%. Find the cost of the antique clock in
(a) 1996,
(b) 1998.

26. A rectangular playground of length 15 m and breadth 5 m has its dimensions increased. If the length is increased by 25% and its width by 15%, calculate the new area. Express this area as a percentage of the original area.

27. A man spends 8% of his monthly salary of $2 500 on himself and 40% of the remainder on his bills and car. He then spends 10% of the remaining on his hobby.
(a) Calculate the amount he spends on his bills and car.
(b) How much does he spend on his hobby in a year?

28. Jenny weighs 58 kg. She weighs 15% more than me. I am 20% heavier than Huimin.
(a) Calculate Huimin's weight and my weight in kilograms.
(b) How much do we both weigh in pounds if 1 kg = 2.224 pounds? Give your answer correct to 2 significant figures.

29. There are 1 500 students in a school. 45% of the students are boys.
(a) What percentage of the students are girls?
(b) How many boys are there in the school?

30. Express 55% as
(a) a decimal,
(b) a fraction in its simplest form.

31. There are 450 people in a housing block. 30% of the people are men, 32% are women and the rest are children.
(a) What is the percentage of children in the housing block?
(b) Calculate the number of women in the housing block?

32. There are 2 310 children in a school. This number is 5% more than it was last year. Calculate the number of children in the school last year.

33. It takes 14 men 125 days to build a house. If the owner wants the house to be built in 50 days, how many more men will be needed?

34. A baker has 2 assistants. The following table shows the number of hours each assistant takes to bake 100 cookies.

	Time taken to bake 100 cookies (h)
Assistant 1	4
Assistant 2	6

Find the time both of them, working together, take to bake 150 cookies.

35. Twelve men take 8 days to dig a well. If the boss wants the digging to be completed in 6 days, how many more men are needed?

36.

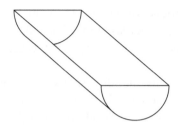

The trough has a semi-circular cross-section of radius 15 cm. It can hold water to a capacity of 3 179.25 cm³. Taking $\pi = 3.14$, calculate
(a) the length of the trough,
(b) the total internal surface area of the trough, assuming that the thickness of the material is negligible.

37. The table shows the number of buns two boys, Xinwei and Yicong, can eat in a given time.

	Number of buns	Time taken/min
Xinwei	5	10
Yicong	2	3

Find the total number of buns they can eat in half an hour.

38. A man works 80 hours in order to earn $3 600. Assuming the same rate of pay per hour, calculate
(a) how much he will earn in 19 hours,
(b) how many hours he will have to work in order to earn $1 170?

39. It takes 6 men to do a job in 2 hours. How many men are needed to do the same job in 3 hours?

40. A machine operator earns $4.80 in 1 hour. Calculate the amount he earns in
(a) $8\frac{1}{2}$ hours,
(b) 35 minutes.

41. A car uses petrol at an average rate of 8.5 litres per 100 km. The owner spends $24.00 on petrol costing 80¢ per litre. Calculate, correct to the nearest kilometre, the distance his car can travel on this amount of petrol.

Time : $\frac{3}{4}$ **hour**

Marks : 40

ALL questions may be attempted.

Answers are to be written on the question paper in the spaces provided.

Omission of essential workings will result in loss of marks. No calculators are allowed.

This paper consists of 12 questions.

1. Find the values of:
    (a) $336 \div 4 \times 7 - 488$ [1]
    (b) $18 + 354 \div 6 - 441 \div 7$ [1]

Ans (a) _____

(b) _____

2. Evaluate each of the following:
    (a) $[-16 \times (12 - 7)] - (-13)$ [2]
    (b) $[(-245) \div (-29 - 6)] \times [-5 - (-2)]$ [2]

Ans (a) _____

(b) _____

3. Evaluate the following and reduce your answers to the lowest terms.

(a) $\dfrac{\dfrac{3}{8} - \dfrac{7}{16}}{\dfrac{1}{4} + \dfrac{5}{8}}$ [2]

(b) $\dfrac{1\dfrac{1}{2} + \dfrac{2}{5} - \dfrac{7}{10}}{3\dfrac{1}{5} - 2\dfrac{3}{10}}$ [2]

Ans (a) _____

(b) _____

4. Find the exact value of each of the following:

(a) $\dfrac{4 \times (5.3 + 7.2)}{5}$ [2]

(b) $\dfrac{7.85 + 6.28 - 4.736}{1.4 \times 5}$ [2]

Ans (a) _____

(b) _____

5. Find the HCF and LCM of:
    (a)   15 and 35   [2]
    (b)   48 and 64   [2]

Ans (a) _____

      (b) _____

6. Simplify the following:
    (a) $5(w + v) - 3(w + 4v)$ [1]

    (b) $\frac{1}{2}(a + 3b) - \frac{3}{4}(4a - 5b)$ [1]

Ans (a) _____

      (b) _____

7. Given that $m = -2$, $n = 3$, $p = 7$ and $q = 10$, evaluate the following:

   (a) $3mn - \dfrac{6p}{q}$ [1]

   (b) $p - (q - m) - (p - n)$ [1]

Ans (a) _____

(b) _____

8. Solve the following equations:

   (a) $12x + 3 = (7x + 4) - (5 - 3x)$ [2]

   (b) $\dfrac{1}{3}(3 - 4x) = \dfrac{1}{2}(x + 13)$ [2]

Ans (a) _____

(b) _____

9. A sum of money is divided in the ratio 2 : 4 : 9. Calculate the smallest share given that the largest share is $45. [3]

Ans _____

10. A minibus leaves town X at 08 30 and arrives in town Y at 13 30 on the same day. Calculate
   (a) the time taken for the journey, [1]
   (b) the average speed of the minibus given that the distance from town X to town Y is 425 km. [3]

Ans (a) _____

   (b) _____

11. Caustic soda contains, by weight, 35% oxygen, $2\frac{1}{2}$% hydrogen and the rest sodium.

Calculate

(a) the percentage of sodium in caustic soda, [1]

(b) the amount of sodium that can be obtained from 120 kg of caustic soda.[3]

Ans (a) _____

(b) _____

12. I bought 8 five-cent stamps, 12 ten-cent stamps and 6 fifty-cent stamps.

(a) How many stamps did I buy altogether? [1]

(b) How much did I pay for the stamps? [2]

Ans (a) _____

(b) _____

MID-TERM ASSESSMENT PAPER 2

Time : $1\frac{1}{2}$ hours

Marks : 60

This paper consists of 2 sections.
Section A consists of **6 questions**.
Section B consists of **5 questions**.
Calculators may be used in this paper. If the degree of accuracy is not specified and if the answer is not exact, the answer should be given to 3 significant figures.

Section A (28 marks)
ALL *questions may be attempted.*

1. **(a)** Evaluate the following, giving your answers correct to 3 significant figures.
    (i) $[256 \div 16 - (586 - 17 \times 30)] \times (23 \times 74 - 1\,539)$ [1]

    (ii) $(\sqrt{676} + 14^2 - \sqrt[3]{512}) \div (11^2 \times 6^3)$ [2]

Ans (i) _____

(ii) _____

51

(b) **(i)** Given the number pattern 60, 47, 36, 27, *a*, *b*, ... , find the value of $b^2 - 4a$. [2]

    (ii) If the number pattern is extended to the left, what is the number just before 60? [1]

Ans (i) _____

(ii) _____

2. At a supermarket, the following purchases are made:
    2 kg of tomatoes at $3.80 per kg
    1.4 kg of bananas at $1.20 per kg
    24 apples at 95¢ for 3
Find the total of the bill. [4]

Ans _____

3. Linda's mother is 7 times her age. Their combined age is 56 years. How old is Linda's mother? [4]

Ans _____

4. 1 kg of rice costs 7 cents more than 1 kg of sugar. If I buy 5 kg of each type and they cost $10.85 altogether, find the cost of 1 kg of rice and 1 kg of sugar respectively. [6]

Ans _____ , _____

5. Ten litres of water are added to 52 litres of milk. Find the percentage of
   (a) pure milk, [2]
   (b) water, [2]
   in the resulting mixture.

Ans (a) ————————————

(b) ————————————

6. In a quadrilateral *ABCD*, the angles *A*, *B* and *C* are in the ratio 1 : 4 : 8 and their sum is 273°. Find
   (a) $\hat{D}$, [2]
   (b) $\hat{C}$. [2]

Ans (a) ————————————

(b) ————————————

Section B (32 marks)
Answer any **FOUR** *questions.*

1. **(a)** Use a calculator to evaluate each of the following, giving your answer correct to 2 decimal places.

    (i) $7.438 \times \left(3\frac{5}{12} - 1.419 + 0.286 \right)$ [1]

    (ii) $\sqrt[3]{38.15^3 - (5.72 + 0.68)^2}$ [1]

Ans (i) _____

(ii) _____

(b) In a school, there are 320 secondary three students. $\frac{3}{5}$ of them are girls. $\frac{2}{3}$ of the girls study 'Accounts' whereas $\frac{1}{4}$ of the boys study 'Accounts'.

    (i) How many girls do not study 'Accounts'?   [3]

    (ii) Find the number of boys who study 'Accounts'.   [3]

Ans (i) _____

(ii) _____

2. (a) Simplify each of the following:

   (i) $9x - 3[4(x - y) + 7(y - x)]$ [1]

   (ii) $\dfrac{3a + b}{2} - \dfrac{a - b}{3} + \dfrac{5a + 7b}{18}$ [1]

Ans (i) ——————————

(ii) ——————————

(b) Solve the following equations:

   (i) $\dfrac{5x + 2}{2x - 3} = \dfrac{2}{7}$ [1]

   (ii) $3(y - 15) - 5(2y - 4) = 12$ [1]

Ans (i) ——————————

(ii) ——————————

(c) Janet has 18 stickers more than Susan and Susan has 4 stickers more than Lin. If they have 62 stickers altogether, find the number of stickers each girl has.

[4]

Ans _____ , _____ , _____

3. (a) David goes shopping and buys some books and stationeries costing $5.83, $3.99, $1.05, $0.85 and $14.37. How much change does he receive from $50?

[2]

Ans _____

(b) Mrs Yeo bought $19\frac{3}{5}$ m of curtain material.

(i) If she used $5\frac{3}{10}$ m of the material for her bedroom, how much material was left? [2]

Ans _____

(ii) If she used $\frac{5}{11}$ of the remainder for the living room, how much material was used for the living room? [2]

Ans _____

(iii) Find how much material was left after using it for the bedroom and living room. [2]

Ans _____

4. (a) The length of the sides of triangle *ABC* are such that *AB* : *BC* : *CA* = 8 : 2 : 5. Calculate the perimeter of triangle *ABC* given that the length of *BC* is 10 cm. [2]

Ans _____

(b) A man earns $2 800 per month. He spends 35% of his earnings on lodging, 5% on transport, 30% on food, 23% on other expenses and saves the rest.
(i) Find the amount of money he uses for lodging and other expenses respectively. [4]
(ii) How much money does he save per month? [2]

Ans (i) _____

(ii) _____

5. **(a)** Express
   (i) 27 632 g in kg and g,   [1]
   (ii) 75 km/h in m/s.   [1]

Ans (i) _____

(ii) _____

(b) A shelf can hold 39 books of thickness 3.5 cm each. If books of thickness 6 cm each are put on the shelf instead, how many books can it hold?   [2]

Ans _____

(c) A racing driver completes a race of 363 km in 3 hours. If he drives at a constant speed,
   (i) how many kilometres will he travel in 48 minutes,   [2]
   (ii) how long will he take to travel 240 km?   [2]

Ans (i) _____

(ii) _____

CHAPTER 8

Solving Problems Involving Financial Transactions

1. A shopkeeper buys an article for $24 and sells it for $30. Find his profit percentage.

2. A bicycle is bought for $128 and sold for $166.40. Calculate the profit and express it as a percentage of the cost price.

3. (a) A manufacturer produced 10 000 similar articles and sold them at $55 per 100 articles. Calculate the total selling price.
   (b) The cost of production for each article was 35 cents. Calculate the total cost of production and express the profit as a percentage of the total cost.

4. (a) Find the simple interest obtained when May invested £1 025 with a bank at 5% per annum for a period of 1 year and 9 months.
   (b) At the end of this period, she withdrew the total amount and exchanged it for Singapore dollars. Find the amount in Singapore dollars. (Take £1 = S$3)

5. (a) When a shopkeeper sells a recorder for $575, he makes a profit of 15%. Calculate the cost price of the recorder.
   (b) The buyer, in turn, sells it at a profit of 20%. Calculate the amount he sells it for.

6. Find the compound interest on $5 500 for 2 years at 6% per annum compounded annually.

7. (a) A man bought a car for $20 500 and sold it three years later for $18 000. Express his loss as a percentage of the cost price.
   (b) He then bought another car for $45 000 and immediately sold it for $57 000. Find his percentage profit.

8. (a) A retailer sold 9 similar articles for $72.54. He made a profit of 20%. Find the cost price of one article.
   (b) A finance company charges a simple interest of 3.5% per year on personal loans. Calculate the total interest paid by a man who borrows $5 000 for 2 years and 6 months.

9. A sales promoter made a mistake in selling an article that was priced at $500 at 15% discount. He had to compensate for the mistake by paying $30. What was the cost price of the article? What should be the marked price if he wanted to make a profit of $55 after giving the same discount of 15%?

10. A company sold some watches to a salesman and made a profit of 25% on each of them. The salesman, in turn, made a profit of 20% when he sold one particular watch for $240. Find the price at which the company sold the watch.

11. A bank exchanges certain currency at the following rate: S$1.70 = US$1.00, S$1.00 = 1.25 yen, S$2.80 = £1.00. Mary has US$5 000 and wishes to change US$3 000 into Japanese yen and the rest into sterling pounds (£). How much of each currency will she have finally?

12. The cost price of a car is $52 000.
    (a) If the discount for cash payment is 12%, how much does the buyer have to pay?
    (b) The car company allows the buyer to pay by monthly instalments at a discount of 8%. If the buyer chooses to pay by 20 monthly instalments, how much will he have to pay each month?

13. A bank pays simple interest at a rate of 5.5% per annum. How much simple interest will I get after 15 months if I have $550 in the bank?

14. Find the compound interest on $2 500 for 30 months at 15% per annum compounded annually. Give your answer to the nearest dollar.

15. A man bought some books for $120. After using them for a year, he sold them to his friend for $95. Calculate his percentage loss. This friend, in turn, sold them at a profit of 25%. Find the price at which his friend sold the books.

16. A sum of $5 000 was deposited with a bank at a certain per cent per annum of interest. It amounted to $6 500 after 2 years. Calculate
    (a) the total interest,
    (b) the per cent per annum interest.

17. A man is trying to decide whether to buy or rent a television set, which costs $1 500. If he buys it, he will receive a discount of 10%. The cost to rent the same set is $30 per month during the first year but a 5% discount is allowed if the year's rental is paid in advance. For the subsequent years, the rental is reduced to $25, but no discount is allowed. If the man wants to rent the set for a maximum of five years, would you advise him to buy or rent it? Explain why.

18. In a sale, a departmental store reduced all its prices by 15%. Calculate
    (a) the cost of an article which was originally priced at $50,
    (b) the original price of an article which was sold in the sale for $212.50.

19. An owner of a boutique wants to sell off the last 10 blouses of the same design. She wants to make a profit of 25% instead of the usual 50%. If she finally sells the blouses at $50, calculate her loss in profit for the 10 blouses.

20. When a man bought 5 similar articles and sold them at a profit of 20%, he earned $160. Given that the amount he paid for one article was the same as his total profit, calculate the selling price of the 5 articles.

21. **(a)** The marked price of a piano is $6 805. A discount of 20% is allowed. What is the selling price?
    (b) If a dealer made a profit of 8% by selling this piano, calculate the cost price of the piano.

22. An article is sold for $830.40 at a profit of 12% on the cost price. Calculate the profit made.

23. **(a)** In a sale, the cost of an article was reduced by 15% to $62.40. Calculate the original cost of the article.
    (b) When a discount of 30% of the marked price of an article is allowed, the article is sold for $140.70. Calculate the discount.

24. A bank pays interest of 5.6% per year. How much interest will be paid on $850 in six months?

25. A man has $600 in a bank which pays simple interest of 4.5% per year.
    (a) How much interest will he get in 3 years?
    (b) After how many years will his interest total $189.00?

26. A shopkeeper makes 22% profit on each article that he sells.
    (a) If an article cost the shopkeeper $20.00, how much does he sell it for?
    (b) If he sells an article for $15.00, how much did it cost him?
    (c) If he makes a profit of $8.00 on an article, how much does he sell it for?

27. The rate of exchange between Singapore dollar and sterling pound is $3.20 to £1.00. Find
    (a) the cost, in Singapore dollars, of a holiday in England which costs £1 300.00,
    (b) the cost, in sterling pounds, of a cruise to Penang which costs $540.00.

28. After a firm had paid tax on the profit it had made, $30 800 000 remained. 30.5% of this sum was set aside for new office buildings.
    (a) Calculate this amount set aside, correct to the nearest $100 000.
    (b) $20 000 000 was paid as dividends to shareholders. Find what percentage this was of the $30 800 000 available, giving your answer correct to 3 significant figures.
    (c) Calculate the amount of tax paid, correct to the nearest $100 000, given that $41\frac{1}{2}\%$ of the profit was paid as tax.

29. A shopkeeper buys 200 apples for $50. He finds that some are bad and throws them away. He sells the remaining apples at 40¢ each, thus making a profit of $22.00. Calculate how many apples were thrown away.

30. Mr Lim went to a bank to change money. The bank exchanges French currency for English currency at the rate of 12 francs to the pound.
    (a) Calculate, in francs, the amount he received in exchange for £26.50.
    (b) Calculate, in pounds, the amount he received in exchange for 90 francs.

31. Janet worked in a company that paid her annual salary in 12 equal monthly instalments. At the end of each year, she was also paid a bonus which amounted to 8% of the value of her total annual sales. Given that her annual salary was $14 400 and that her total sales during the first year amounted to $30 000, calculate

    (a) her monthly salary,

    (b) her total income in her first year.

32. Mr Tan, Mr Yong and Mr Ng each decided to buy a new car which was priced in the showroom at $120 000.

    (a) Mr Tan offered his old car in exchange and the salesman allowed him $56 000 off the cost of the new car. Calculate how much more Mr Tan had to pay for his new car.

    (b) Mr Yong paid for his new car in cash and was given a discount. Given that he paid $108 000 for his new car, calculate the percentage discount he received.

    (c) Mr Ng agreed to pay 60% of the showroom price of the car as a deposit and the balance in equal monthly instalments over a period of 5 years. Calculate the amount of each monthly instalment.

    (d) The salesman had hoped to sell each new car for $120 000 so that he could make a profit of 20% on the cost price. Calculate the cost price of each new car.

CHAPTER 9

Introducing Geometry

1. Find the value of x in the following diagrams where AB is a straight line.

(a)
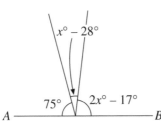

(b)
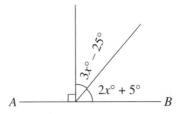

(c)
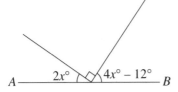

(d)
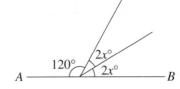

(e)

(f)
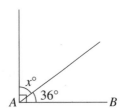

2. Find the value of x and of y in the following diagrams.

(a)
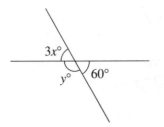

(b)
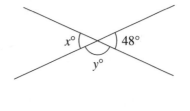

(c)

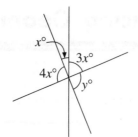

(d)

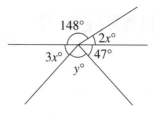

(e)

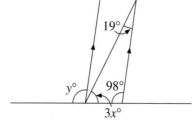

3. Form an equation in x and solve it.

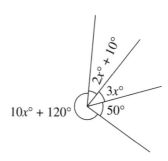

4. Form an equation in x and find its value.

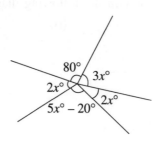

5. Form an equation in x and solve it.

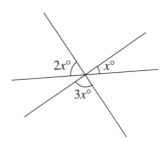

6. Find the values of x, y and z in the following diagrams.

(a)

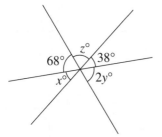

(b)

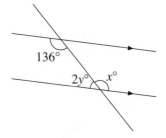

(c)

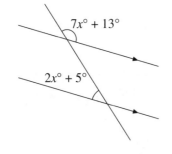

(d)

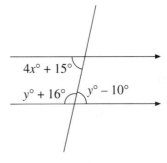

(e)

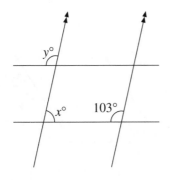

(f)

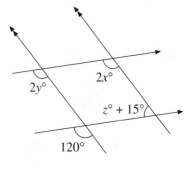

7. Calculate the value of x in each of the following diagrams.

(a)

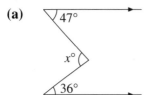

(b)

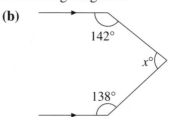

(c)

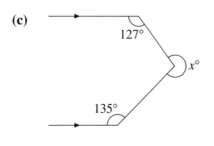

(d)

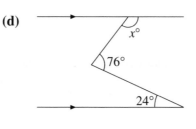

(e)

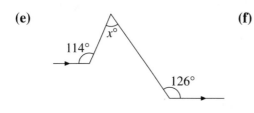

(f)

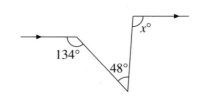

(g)

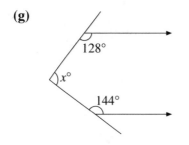

(h)

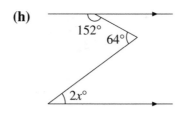

(i)

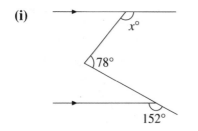

(j)

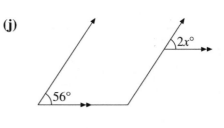

8. Find the value of *x*.

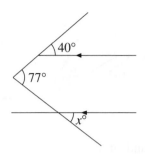

9. Find the value of *x*.

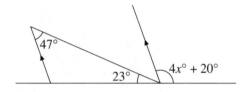

10. Find the value of *a* and of *b*.

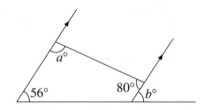

11. In the diagram, *FED* is parallel to *ABC*.
Calculate

(a) $F\hat{E}B$,

(b) $E\hat{D}G$.

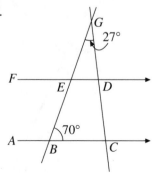

12. Form an equation in x and solve it.

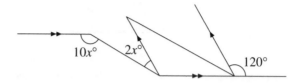

13. Calculate the value of x and of y.

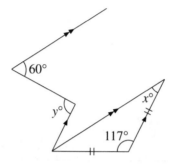

14. Find the value of x and of y.

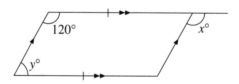

15. Find the value of x and of y.

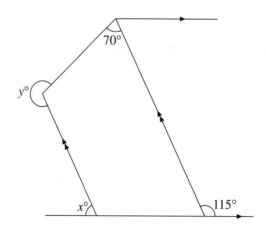

16. Find the values of x and y.

(a)

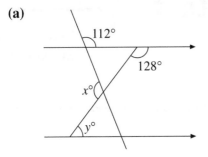

(b)

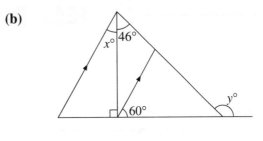

(c)

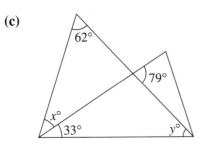

(d)

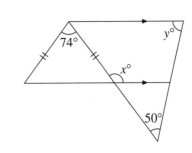

17. Draw a line segment AB, of length 7.4 cm. Construct a perpendicular bisector of AB.

18. Draw a line segment XY, of length 12.8 cm. Mark on XY, a point A, 5.8 cm from X. Draw a perpendicular to XY through A.

19. Draw the triangle ABC accurately with the given measurements. Construct the perpendicular bisector of AB and of BC. Mark with the letter X, the point where these two perpendicular bisectors meet.

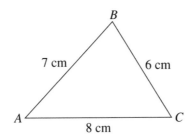

Time : 1 hour

Marks : 50

1. **(a)** A man pays $33.20 for 7 dozens of drinks and sells them at 45 cents each. Find the percentage profit. [3]

Ans _____

(b) A bank pays interest of 5.2% per year. How much interest will be paid on $2 500.00 in 2 years and 9 months? [3]

Ans _____

2. A shopkeeper makes a profit of 18% if he sells an article for $68.00.

    (a) Calculate the cost price of the article. [2]

    (b) If the shopkeeper allows $7\frac{1}{2}\%$ off for cash payment, calculate

        (i) the cash price of the article, [2]

        (ii) his percentage profit for a cash sale. [3]

Ans (a) _____

    (b) (i) _____

        (ii) _____

3. A bank exchanges American currency for British currency at the rate of 1.70 dollars ($) to the pound (£).

(a) Calculate, in dollars, the amount received for £200. [2]

(b) Calculate, in pounds, the amount paid for $750 by a customer who also had to pay an extra 2% commission for this transaction. [4]

Ans (a) _____

(b) _____

4. (a) A man is trying to decide whether to buy or to rent a new television set. The model he wants costs $950.00 and the dealer charges an additional $2\frac{1}{2}\%$ of this cost to install it. During the first year, no charge will be made for repairs. After this the man estimates that repairs will cost $30 for each of the next four years, and then $45 for each of the following three years. At the end of these eight years, he expects to receive a trade-in value of $100.00 for the set when he buys a new one. Calculate

    (i) the installation charge,   [1]

    (ii) the total estimated repair cost,   [2]

    (iii) the estimated net cost of the set over the eight years (that is the total he expects to pay less the trade-in value).   [2]

Ans (i) _____

(ii) _____

(iii) _____

(b) The cost to rent the same set is $18.50 per month during the first year but $7\frac{1}{2}\%$ discount is allowed if the year's rental is paid in advance. Calculate the rental for this year if it is paid in advance. [2]

Ans _____

(c) For the second and the subsequent years, the rental is reduced to $15.50 per month but no discount is allowed.
  (i) Calculate the rental for the second year. [1]
  (ii) Hence calculate the total rental if the set is kept for eight years, with the first year's rental being paid in advance. [2]

Ans (i) _____

(ii) _____

5. The table shows the cost of electricity.

Usage		Cost
1st	80 kW/h	0.25 cents per kW/h
Next	100 kW/h	0.35 cents per kW/h

(a) Calculate the cost of using 175 kW/h of electricity. [3]

(b) If the cost is $41.70, how much electricity is used? [3]

Ans (a) _____

(b) _____

6. In the diagram, AB is parallel to CD, $A\hat{B}E = 76°$ and $C\hat{D}E = 43°$. Find $B\hat{E}A$.
[3]

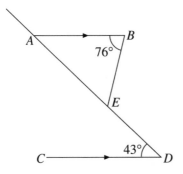

Ans _____

7. In the diagram, XYZ is a straight line and XW is parallel to YV. Given that $V\hat{Y}Z = 2x° + 26°$, $W\hat{Y}X = 3x° - 2°$ and $X\hat{W}Y = x°$, find the value of x and hence find $W\hat{X}Y$. [4]

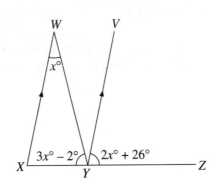

Ans $x =$ _____

$W\hat{X}Y =$ _____

8. (a) Find the value of x and of y in the following diagrams. [4]

(i)

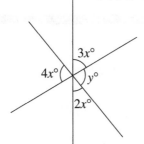

(ii)

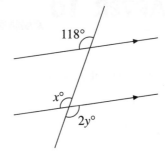

Ans (i) _____

(ii) _____

(b) Draw a line PQ of length 10.6 cm. Using a ruler and a pair of compasses only, construct the perpendicular bisector of PQ. [4]

1. Find the values of x, y and z in the following diagrams.

(a)
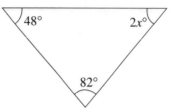

(b)
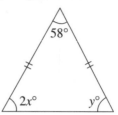

(c)
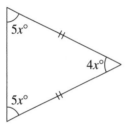

(d)
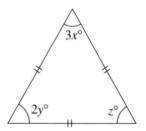

(e)
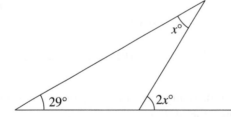

2. Form an equation in x and solve it.

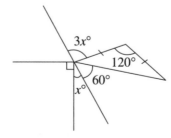

3.

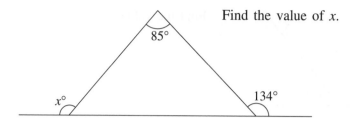

Find the value of x.

4.

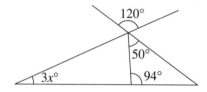

Find the value of x.

5.

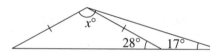

Find the value of x.

6.

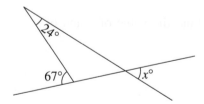

Find the value of x.

7.

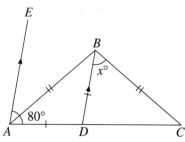

In the diagram, *AE* is parallel to *DB*. If *AD* = *DB* and *AB* = *BC*, find the value of *x*.

8.

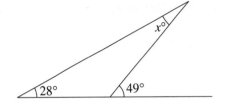

Find the value of *x*.

9.

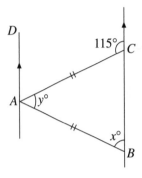

Find the value of *x* and of *y*, given that *AB* = *AC* and *AD* is parallel to *BC*.

10.

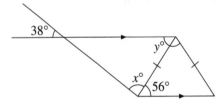

Find the value of *x* and of *y*.

11.

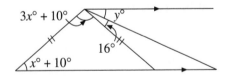

Find the value of *x* and of *y*.

12.

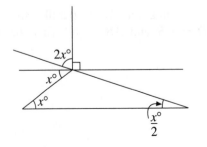

Find the value of *x*.

13. Calculate the values of x, y and z in the following diagrams.

(a)

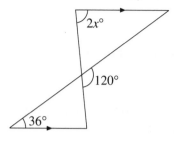

(b)

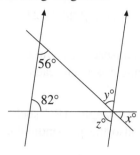

(c)

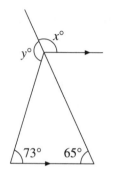

(d)

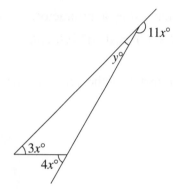

14. The angles of a triangle are $2n°$, $3n°$ and $3n°$.
   (a) Name the kind of triangle that has these angles.
   (b) Find the value of n.

15. Construct a triangle PQR such that $PQ = 5$ cm, $PR = 4$ cm and $\hat{P} = 120°$. Measure $\hat{R}$.

16. Construct a triangle ABC such that $BC = 6.2$ cm, $A\hat{B}C = 37°$ and $A\hat{C}B = 42°$.

17. Construct a triangle ABC in which $AB = 7$ cm, $B\hat{A}C = A\hat{B}C = 50°$. Measure and write down the length of AC.

18. Construct a triangle PQR such that $PQ = 5.3$ cm, $QR = 4$ cm and $PR = 5.3$ cm. Construct also the angle bisector of $P\hat{Q}R$.

19. In the diagram, $QP = QS = QR$, $S\hat{Q}R = 78°$ and PS is parallel to QR. Calculate the value of
   (a) x,
   (b) y.

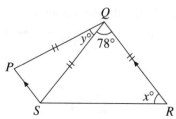

20. Using only ruler and compasses, construct triangle ABC such that $AB = 5$ cm, $B\hat{A}C = 30°$ and $A\hat{B}C = 45°$.

21. Construct an isosceles right-angled triangle, given that the two sides which enclosed the right angle is 6 cm each.

22. Construct a triangle ABC such that $AB = 5$ cm, $BC = 4$ cm and $AC = 4.5$ cm. Construct also the perpendicular bisector of AB.

23. Without using a protractor, construct a triangle ABC such that $AB = 4$ cm, $A\hat{B}C = 60°$ and $AC = 6$ cm.

24. Given that O is the centre of the circle, find the value of x and of y.

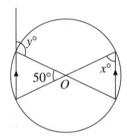

25. A polygon has n sides. Three of the exterior angles are $23°$, $35°$ and $62°$, while each of the remaining $(n - 3)$ exterior angles is $30°$. Find the value of n.

26. Calculate the values of x, y and z in the following kites.

(a)

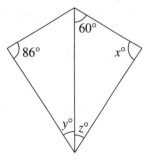

(b)

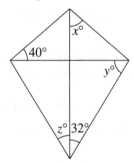

27. Calculate the values of x, y and z in the following parallelograms.

(a)

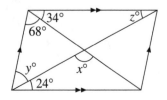

(b)

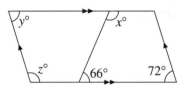

84

28.

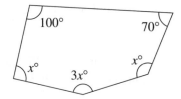

Find the value of x.

29.

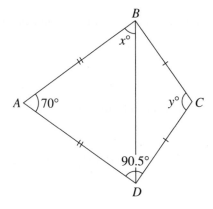

Find the value of x and of y where $ABCD$ is a kite.

30.

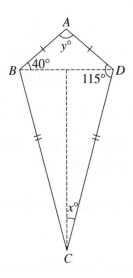

In the diagram, $ABCD$ is a kite. Find the value of x and of y.

31. **(a)** Find the size of each interior angle of a regular polygon with 18 sides.
   (b) Find the number of sides of a regular polygon whose exterior angle is 15°.

32. **(a)** Calculate the size of each exterior angle of a regular polygon with 20 sides.
   (b) Four of the interior angles of a 12-sided polygon are $(x - 10)°$ each and the remaining interior angles are 160° each. Calculate the value of x.

33. A polygon has n sides. Two of its interior angles are $70°$ and $80°$. The remaining interior angles are each $30°$. Calculate the value of n.

34. **(a)** Find the number of sides of a polygon whose interior angle is $135°$ each.
(b) Calculate the size of an exterior angle of a regular polygon with 32 sides.

35. The interior angles of a pentagon are $3x°$, $2x°$, $x°$, $4x°$ and $5x°$ respectively. Find the value of x.

36. Two interior angles of a polygon are $50°$ and $62°$. The rest of the interior angles are $x°$, $2x°$ and $5x°$. Find
(a) the number of sides of the polygon,
(b) the value of x.

37. Find the number of sides of a regular polygon if each interior angle is 17 times its exterior angle.

38. The exterior angles of a quadrilateral are $2x°$, $3x°$, $95°$ and $115°$. Calculate
(a) the value of x,
(b) the largest interior angle.

39. Construct a quadrilateral $ABCD$ such that $AB = 3.2$ cm, $BC = 4.8$ cm, $AD = 6.9$ cm, $A\hat{B}C = 90°$ and $B\hat{C}D = 115°$.

40. Construct a quadrilateral $ABCD$ such that $AD = CD = 46$ mm, $AB = 40$ mm, $BC = 33$ mm and $D\hat{A}B = 80°$. Construct also the angle bisector of $A\hat{B}C$.

41. **(a)** The interior angles of a quadrilateral are in the ratio $3 : 4 : 6 : 7$. Calculate the smallest interior angle of this quadrilateral.
(b) Each exterior angle of a regular polygon with 20 sides is $x°$, while that of a regular polygon with n sides is $(x + 12)°$. Calculate the value of n.

42. Construct, without using a protractor, a parallelogram $PQRS$ such that $P\hat{Q}R = 60°$, $PQ = 5$ cm and $QR = 6$ cm.

43. Construct a square $ABCD$ of side 5 cm. Construct also the angle bisector of $A\hat{B}C$.

44. Construct a parallelogram $ABCD$ where $AB = 6$ cm, $AD = 4$ cm and $D\hat{A}B = 55°$.

45. Construct a rectangle whose sides are equal to 5.6 cm and 7.4 cm. Measure and write down the length of the diagonal.

46. Construct a rhombus $ABCD$ of side 6.4 cm and $A\hat{B}C = 74°$. Measure and write down the length of AC and of BD.

1. Indicate by dotted lines and write down the number of lines of symmetry of the following figures.

   (a)

   (b)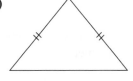

   (c)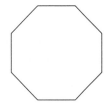

2. The figure has a horizontal line of symmetry.
   (a) Complete the full figure.
   (b) The complete figure has another line of symmetry. Draw the line of symmetry.

   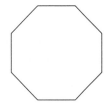

3.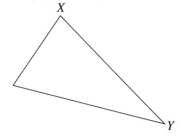

   The diagram shows a piece of paper which has been folded along its line of symmetry *XY*. Complete the diagram to show the original shape of the piece of paper.

4. Use your geometrical instruments to complete each of the following figures to form a symmetrical figure with respect to the line *l*.

   (a)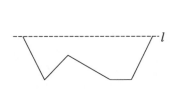

   (b)

(c)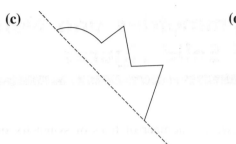

(d)

5. For each of the following figures, show with dotted lines the lines of symmetry and state the number of lines of symmetry.

(a) 　　**(b)** 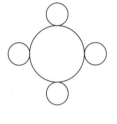　　**(c)**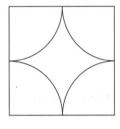

6. Using the least number of lines, complete the following diagram so that the shape has only 2 lines of symmetry.

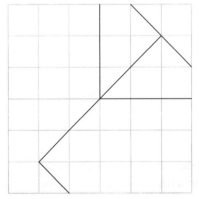

7. For each of the following figures, draw the lines of symmetry. State also the number of axes of rotational symmetry.

(a) 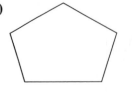　　**(b)** 　　**(c)**

8. The square bathroom tile shown has a vertical and horizontal symmetry. Complete the shading to show the full pattern.

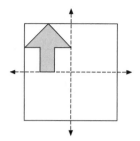

9. Name a quadrilateral which has in its own plane, exactly
   (a) 1 axis of symmetry,
   (b) 2 axes of symmetry,
   (c) 4 axes of symmetry.

10. Draw the lines of symmetry of the following figures. State also the order of rotational symmetry.
    (a)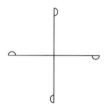
    (b)
    (c)

11. Draw the lines of symmetry for the following figures. State also the order of rotational symmetry.
    (a)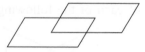
    (b)

    (c)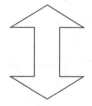

12. Each of the following figures has rotational symmetry about an axis, what is the order of symmetry of each figure?
    (a)
    (b)
    (c)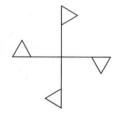

13. 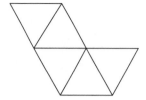 Add one equilateral triangle to the figure to make it have rotational symmetry.

14. Add 3 lines to the following diagram so that the shape has rotational symmetry of the order 4 about O, the centre of the circle.

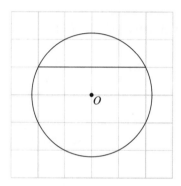

15. Write down the order of rotational symmetry of each of the following shapes.

(a) 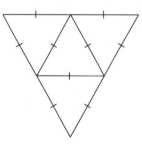   **(b)**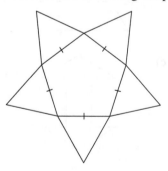

(c)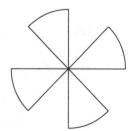

16. State the number of planes of symmetry and axes of rotational symmetry of the following figures.

(a)

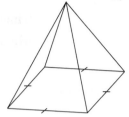

(b)

17. Draw 2 planes of symmetry for each of the following figures and state the number of axes of rotational symmetry.

(a)

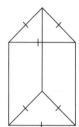

(b)

(c)

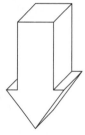

18. Name the geometrical shapes of the following objects.
   (a) a can of sardines
   (b) a basketball
   (c) a shoe box
   (d) an ice-cream cornet (unfilled)

19. Draw 2 planes of symmetry for each of the following solids.

(a)

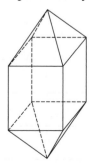

(b)

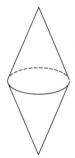

TEST PAPER 5

Time : 1 hour

Marks : 50

1. Calculate the values of *x*, *y* and *z* in the following diagrams. [10]

    (a)

    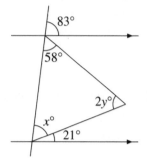

    (b)

    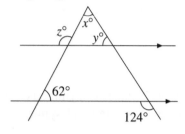

    (c)

    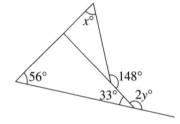

    (d)

    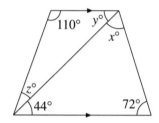

    Ans (a) _____

    (b) _____

    (c) _____

    (d) _____

2. Calculate the values of x, y and z in the following rectangles. [6]

(a)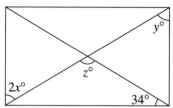

(b)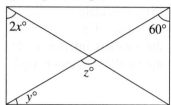

Ans (a) _____

(b) _____

3. The exterior angles of a pentagon are $2x°$, $(2x + 3)°$, $(3x + 12)°$, $(3x - 20)°$ and $(x + 35)°$. Calculate
   (a) the value of x, [1]
   (b) the smallest interior angle, [2]
   (c) the smallest exterior angle. [2]

Ans (a) _____

(b) _____

(c) _____

4. Construct $\triangle XYZ$ such that $Y\hat{X}Z = 90°$, $XY = 6$ cm and $XZ = 3.5$ cm. Construct the perpendicular bisector of XY and let it cut YZ at M. Measure and write down the length of YM. [6]

Ans _____

5. For each of the following figures,
- **(i)** draw all the lines of symmetry (if any),
- **(ii)** write down the number of lines of symmetry (if any),
- **(iii)** state the order of rotational symmetry (if any) and mark with a cross (✗) the centre of rotational symmetry where possible. [6]

(a)

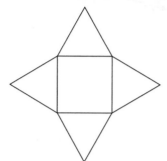

(b)

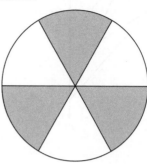

Ans (a) (ii) _____

  (iii) _____

(b) (ii) _____

  (iii) _____

(c) (ii) _____

  (iii) _____

6. Complete each of the following figures to form a symmetrical figure with respect to the line m. [8]

(a)

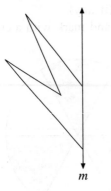

m

(b)

m

(c)

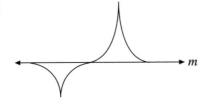

m

(d)

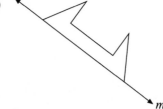

m

7. State the number of planes of symmetry and the number of axes of rotational symmetry for the following solids. [4]

(a)

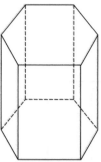

A regular right
hexagonal prism

(b)

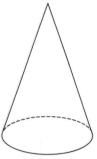

A right circular
cone

Ans (a) _____

(b) _____

8. Name the solid that can be formed by the following net. Draw a sketch for this solid. [5]

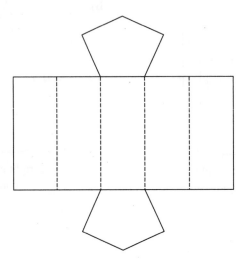

Ans _____

CHAPTER 12 / Area and Perimeter

1. Find the perimeter of a square board if its area is 8 100 cm².

2. Find the perimeter of a rectangular table top if its area is 24 500 cm² and its width is 140 cm.

3. Find the base of a triangle whose area and height are 64 cm² and 8 cm respectively.

4. The area of a square is 1 024 cm².
   (a) What is the length of the square?
   (b) Calculate the perimeter of the square.

5. Find the height of a trapezium if its area is 208 cm² and its parallel sides are 15 cm and 17 cm.

6. Find the radius of a circle whose circumference is 59.7 cm.

7. Fifi's bicycle has wheels of radius 30 cm.
   (a) Calculate the circumference of Fifi's front wheel. (Take $\pi = 3.142$)
   (b) Calculate the distance Fifi cycles when the front wheel rotates 80 times, giving your answer correct to the nearest centimetre.

8. The figure shown is $\frac{3}{5}$ of the entire circle. Taking π to be $\frac{22}{7}$, and the radius of the circle to be 21 cm, find the perimeter of the figure.

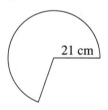

21 cm

9. The radii of the two circles are 56 mm and 48 mm. Taking π to be 3.14, calculate the shaded area.

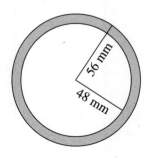

56 mm

48 mm

10. Calculate the shaded areas of the following diagrams.

(a)

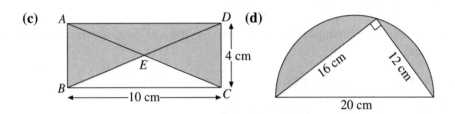

13 cm

(b)

2 cm

4 cm

8 cm

5 cm

3 cm

(c)

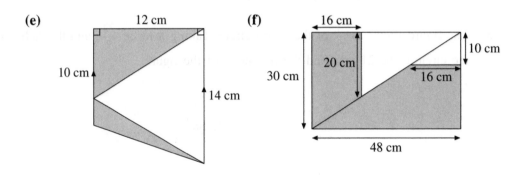

A   D

4 cm

E

B   C

10 cm

(d)

16 cm   12 cm

20 cm

(e)

12 cm

10 cm

14 cm

(f)

16 cm

20 cm

10 cm

30 cm

16 cm

48 cm

(g)

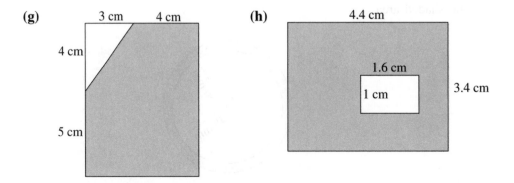

3 cm   4 cm

4 cm

5 cm

(h)

4.4 cm

1.6 cm

1 cm

3.4 cm

11. Find the area of each of the diagrams (dimensions are in cm).

(a)
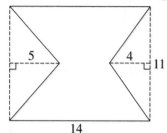

(b)
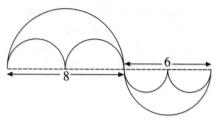

(c)
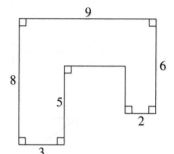

(d)
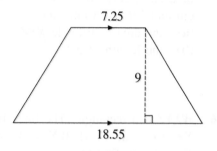

12. A plot of land in the shape of a square of side 3 km is converted into a park. Two corners of the park in the shape of a quadrant of radius 1.5 km are converted into playgrounds. Taking $\pi = 3.14$, calculate
(a) the total area of the two playgrounds,
(b) the perimeter of the remaining park.

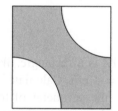

13.

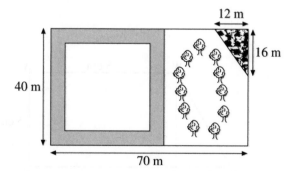

The sketch shows a garden plot 70 m by 40 m. It has a square lawn surrounded by a path 1 m wide (shaded). It also has a triangular flower bed with sides 20 m, 12 m and 16 m. Find
(a) the area of the whole plot,
(b) the area of the path,
(c) the area of the triangular flower bed.

14. **ABCD** is a rectangle. Given that $AB = (4x + 6)$ cm, $BC = (x - 4)$ cm and that the perimeter of the rectangle is 56 cm, find the value of x.

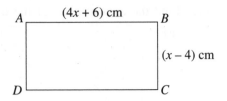

15. In the diagram, XA and YB are altitudes of triangle XYZ. If $XZ = 5$ cm, $YZ = 8$ cm and $YB = 7.5$ cm, find
    (a) the area of triangle XYZ,
    (b) the length of XA.

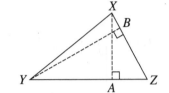

16. **WXYZ** is a rectangle. The lines WY and XZ cross at V. If $WX = 4$ cm and $XY = 6$ cm, find the area of
    (a) triangle WXY,
    (b) triangle WZV.

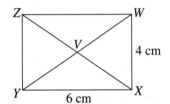

17. **WXYZ** is a rectangle. $WX = 6.5$ cm and $WZ = 4$ cm. Calculate
    (a) the perimeter of the rectangle,
    (b) the area of triangle XYZ.

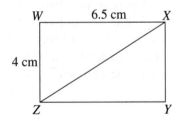

18.

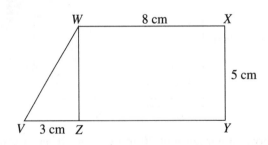

WXYZ is a rectangle and YZV is a straight line. $WX = 8$ cm, $XY = 5$ cm and $VZ = 3$ cm. Calculate
(a) the area of triangle WZV,
(b) the area of quadrilateral $WXYV$.

19. *APC* is a semicircle centred at *B*. Given that *PB* = 12 cm and *BR* = 5 cm, calculate
    (a) the perimeter of the shaded region *APQ*,
    (b) the area of the shaded region.
    (Leave your answers in terms of π)

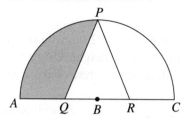

20. A piece of card is cut into the shape shown in the diagram. *BCD* is a circular arc, centre *O*, with circle *CEOF* enclosed. If *OB* = 3 cm, calculate
    (a) the area of the shaded region,
    (b) the total length of the boundary of the shaded region.

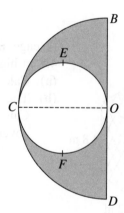

21. A patch of land in the shape of a quadrant of radius 4.2 m has a path of width 0.7 m running parallel to its edge. Find
    (a) the area of the path,
    (b) the area not covered by the path.

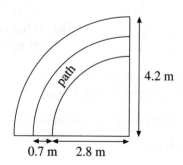

CHAPTER 13

Volume, Surface Area and Density

1. A rectangular prism with a base of 20 cm by 0.8 m and height 50 cm is recast to form a solid cylinder of the same height. Using a calculator, find the radius of the cylinder correct to 3 significant figures. (Take $\pi = 3.14$)

2.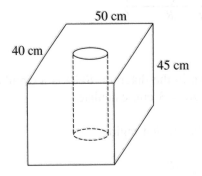

   A cylindrical hole of radius 10 cm is drilled through a rectangular prism of base 50 cm by 40 cm and height 45 cm. Find, using a calculator, the volume of the remaining solid. (Take $\pi = 3.142$)

3.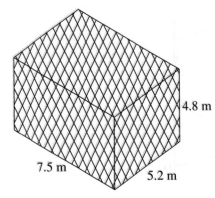

   A cage is 7.5 m long, 5.2 m wide and 4.8 m high.
   (a) Calculate the volume of the cage.
   (b) The cage does not have a base. Calculate the area of netting needed to cover the cage.

4.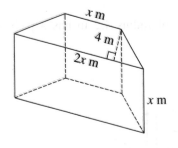

   The figure shows a water tank with a base in the shape of a trapezium. The two parallel sides are x metres and $2x$ metres long. The height of the tank is x metres.
   (a) Show that the volume of the tank is $6x^2$ m^3.
   (b) What value of x will give a volume of 96 m^3?

5. A piece of cake takes the shape of half a cylinder of diameter 14 cm and height 10 cm.

   Taking π to be $\dfrac{22}{7}$, find the total surface area of the cake and its volume.

   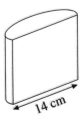

6. A cylindrical tank of radius 5 m and height 10 m is filled with water to a height of 7 m. Taking π to be 3.14, find the volume of the cylinder which is not occupied by water.

7. Calculate
    (a) the volume of the solid,
    (b) the total surface area of the solid.

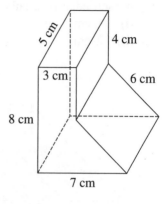

8. A circular cylinder has a radius of 7 cm and a height of 13 cm. Taking π to be 3.14, calculate
    (a) the area of the circular base,
    (b) the volume of the cylinder.

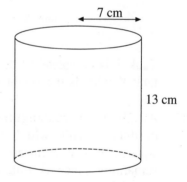

9. A closed rectangular box has a square base $ABCD$ of side x cm and a height y cm.
    (a) Find the total surface area of the box.
    (b) If the volume of the box is 100 cm^3, evaluate x if $y = 5$.

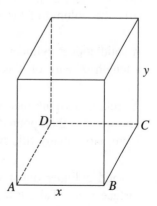

105

10. A rectangular block measures 20 cm by 12 cm by 4 cm.

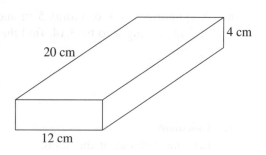

(a) Calculate the total surface area of the block.

(b) Calculate the number of cubes which can be made from the block if each edge of a cube measures

    (i) 1 cm,

    (ii) 2 cm.

11.

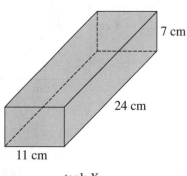

tank *X*

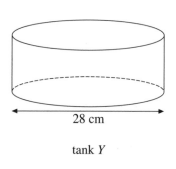

tank *Y*

Tank *X* is completely filled with water. If all the water in tank *X* is poured into tank *Y*, what is the height of the water in tank *Y*?

12. *ABCD* is a rectangular piece of cardboard from which four shaded squares of side 2 cm are cut off. The remaining piece is folded along the dotted lines to form a rectangular box with *EFGH* as its base. If *BC* = 15 cm and *AB* = 6 cm, calculate

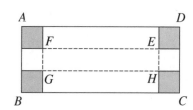

(a) the area of the base *EFGH*,

(b) the volume of the box.

13. A solid copper cylinder of diameter 7 cm is 14 cm long. It is melted and recast into a length of wire of diameter 0.3 cm. Find the length of the wire.

14. A rectangular tank measuring 30 cm by 20 cm contains water to a depth of 18 cm. The water is then poured into cylindrical glasses each of diameter 5 cm and height 7 cm. How many full cylindrical glasses can be filled?

15. A solid cylinder has a volume of 5 024 cm^3. If its radius is 8 cm, find its total surface area. (Take $\pi = 3.14$)

16. Find the volume and total surface area of each of the following solids. All dimensions given are in cm.

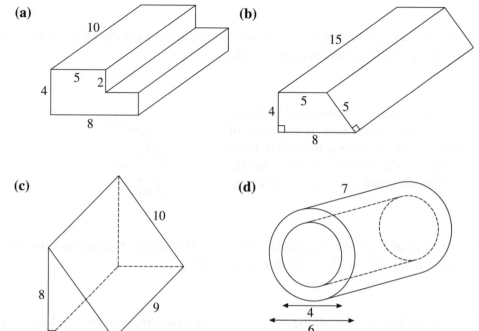

(a)

10
5 2
4
8

(b)

15
5
4 5
8

(c)

10
8
9
6

(d)

7
4
6

(e)

2
4
4
5   3
3
10

(f)

1
2
5
2   2
2
6

17. A closed rectangular wooden box is made of wood of thickness 0.5 cm. Its external dimensions are 30 cm by 22 cm by 12 cm. Find
(a) its internal dimensions,
(b) its external volume,
(c) its internal volume,
(d) the volume of wood needed in making the box,
(e) the mass of the empty box if the density of the wood used is 1.2 kg/m^3.

18. A plastic cube of side 9 cm is melted down and remade into a cuboid with a square base of side 18 cm. Calculate the height of this new cuboid.

19. A cylindrical tree stump of radius 1 m and height 50 cm is sawn into 5 equal pieces. Calculate the volume of each piece in m³. (Take $\pi = 3.14$)

20. A gold ingot in the shape of a cuboid of sides 6 cm by 3 cm by 2 cm has a mass of 695 g. Calculate the density of gold.

21. A plastic tubing is cylindrical in shape. It has three cylindrical holes, each of radius 1.4 mm, running through it. If the length of the tubing is 8 cm, find the volume of plastic, in cm³, in the tubing.

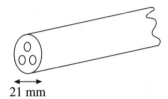

21 mm

22. The tyre of a car has a diameter of 63 cm. How many revolutions does the tyre make if the car travels a distance of 9.9 km?

23. A man wants to paint all the walls of a room measuring 8 m by 5 m by 4 m. Find the surface area of the walls that need to be painted.

24. Ali has a fish tank measuring 28 cm by 16 cm by 20 cm. He wished to fill it full with water. Calculate the amount of water, in cm³, needed to be poured into the tank.

25. Calculate the volume of the solid below. (Take $\pi = \frac{22}{7}$)

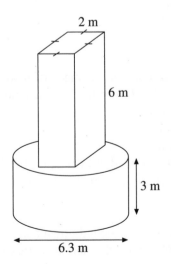

2 m

6 m

3 m

6.3 m

26. A hollow aluminium cylinder of diameter 3.5 m and height 8 m is unrolled to form a rectangular sheet. Calculate the area of the rectangular sheet. (Take $\pi = \frac{22}{7}$)

27. Mr Lim wished to paint a tunnel of sides 4 m, length 10 m and thickness 0.5 m as shown in the diagram. If only the outer and inner surfaces have to be painted, find this area.

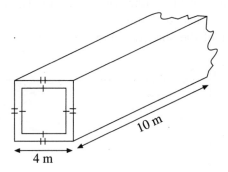

TEST PAPER 6

Time : 1 hour

Marks : 50

1. The diagram shows a rectangle *WXYZ* and a semicircle with diameter *XY* and centre *O*. The radius of the semicircle is 3.2 cm. Taking π to be 3.14, calculate
    (a) the area of the shaded figure,   [3]
    (b) the perimeter of the shaded figure.   [3]

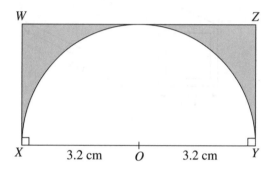

Ans (a) _____

(*b*) _____

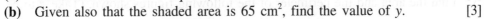

2. **(a)** Given that *ABCD* is a square, find the value of *x*. [2]
  (b) Given also that the shaded area is 65 cm², find the value of *y*. [3]

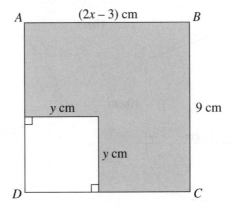

Ans (a) _____

(b) _____

3. Find the area and the perimeter of the following figures shown. (Take π to be $\frac{22}{7}$)

[8]

(a)

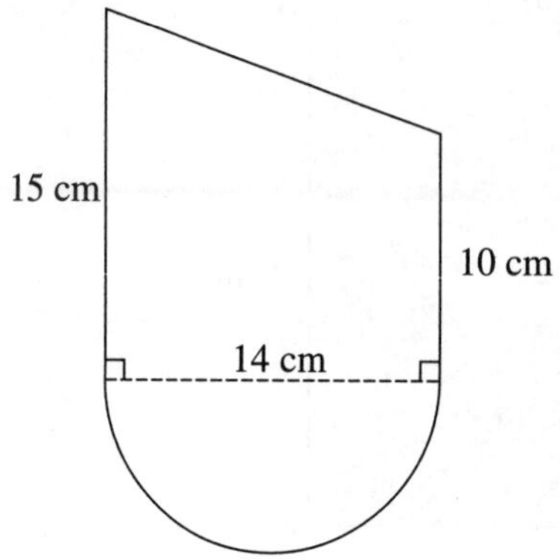

15 cm

10 cm

14 cm

(b)

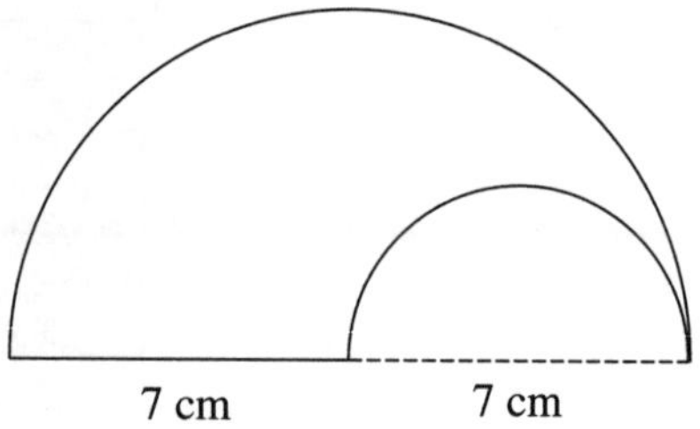

7 cm   7 cm

Ans (a) _____

(b) _____

4. A jogging track has the shape as shown. What distance would David cover if he jogs $5\frac{1}{2}$ rounds on the track? (Take $\pi = \frac{22}{7}$) [5]

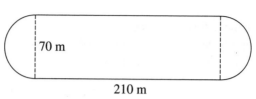

70 m

210 m

Ans _____

5. A rectangular envelope 18 cm by 9.5 cm has two rectangular stamps each of length 30 mm and breadth 18 mm. Find the area of the face of the envelope not covered by the stamps. [5]

Ans _____

6. The square base of a box measures 360 mm by 360 mm. The sides of the box are made from wood which is 6 mm thick and 100 mm wide. Mr Wong buys 1.5 m of this wood to make the sides of the box. The wood costs $3.25 per metre. Calculate

(a) the cost of the 1.5 m of wood, [2]
(b) the total length needed for the sides of the box, [3]
(c) the length, in mm, of wood left over. [3]

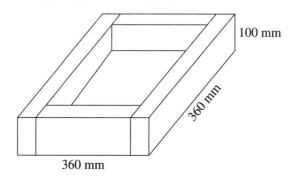

Ans (a) _____

(b) _____

(c) _____

7. (a) Find the volume of the given solid, taking π to be 3.142. [4]

(b) Given that the solid is made from metal of density 6 g/cm³, find its mass.

[2]

Ans (a) _____

(b) _____

8. A packet of soap powder is a cuboid of length 16 cm, breadth 5 cm and height 25 cm.

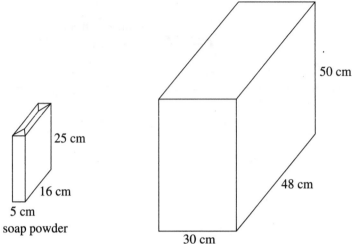

25 cm

16 cm

5 cm

soap powder

50 cm

48 cm

30 cm

(a) Calculate the volume of the packet of soap powder. [2]
(b) Calculate the number of packets of soap powder which can be placed in a rectangular box of length 48 cm, breadth 30 cm and height 50 cm. [5]

Ans (a) _____

(b) _____

1. Triangles *ABC* and *XYZ* are similar. Find the value of *a* and of *b*.

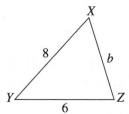

2. Given that $\triangle ABC$ and $\triangle DEF$ are similar, find the length of *BC* and of *DF*.

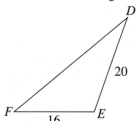

3. Given that the two triangles are similar, form an equation in *x* and solve it.

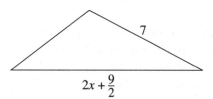

4. Given that the two triangles below are similar, find the value of *x*.

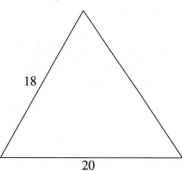

117

5. Find the values of XY, YZ and $B\hat{A}C$.

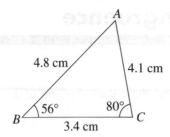 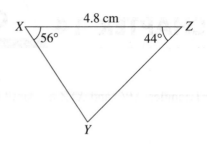

6. In the diagram, AB is parallel to CD.
$AE = 3$ cm, $ED = 5$ cm and $BE = 2.5$ cm. Find
(a) the ratio $AB : CD$,
(b) the length of CE.

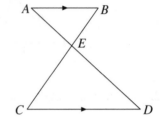

7. In the diagram, AB is parallel to ED,
$ED = 5$ cm, $AB = 15$ cm and $EC = 7$ cm. Find
the length of BE.

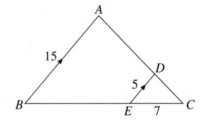

8. In the diagram, AB is parallel to CD,
$AE = 4$ cm, $BE = 6$ cm and $ED = 10$ cm. Find
(a) the length of CE,
(b) the value of the ratio $AB : CD$.

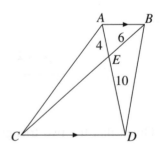

9. In the diagram, BC is parallel to DE.
$AB = 6$ cm, $BD = 2$ cm, $AC = (x + 5)$ cm and
$CE = x$ cm. Find the value of x.

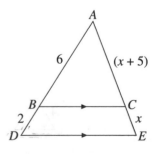

10. In the diagram, *ABCD* is a plot of land in the shape of a trapezium of height 9 cm and parallel sides 7 cm and 12 cm. If the actual length of *AB* is 14 km, find
(a) the actual length of *CD* and of *AE*,
(b) the actual area of *ABCD*.

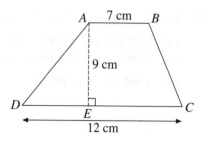

11. Find the value of *x*.

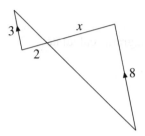

12. In triangle *ADE*, *AB* : *BD* = 3 : 2.
(a) If the length of *BC* = 4 cm, find the length of *DE*.
(b) Find the length of *CE* if *AC* = 12 cm.

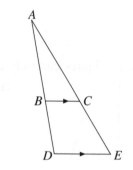

13. In the diagram, *BC* is parallel to *DE*. Given that *DE* = 21 cm, *BC* = 6 cm and *AC* = 2 cm, find
(a) *CE*,
(b) *AB* : *AD*.

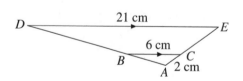

14. In the diagram, *AD* = 6 cm and *DE* = 8 cm. Find
(a) *AB* : *AC*,
(b) *FG* : *AG*.

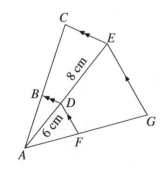

15. In the diagram, $AB = 27$ cm, $AE = 35$ cm, $BE = 22.5$ cm, $DE = 4.5$ cm, $CD = 35$ cm and $A\hat{B}D = 90°$.

(a) Write down the triangles that are congruent.

(b) Find BC and $B\hat{C}D$.

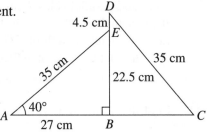

16. Using the dimensions in the diagram, calculate

(a) DE,

(b) the ratio $AD : AB$.

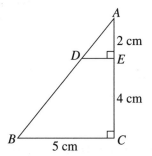

17. Study the figures carefully and name those that are congruent.

(a)

(b)

(c)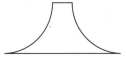

(d)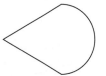

(e)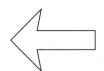

(f)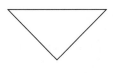

(g)

(h)

(i)

(j)

18. Find the value of x and of y.

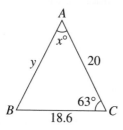 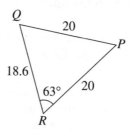

19.

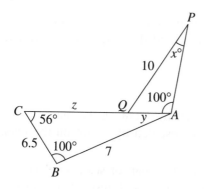

Triangles ABC and PAQ are congruent. Find the value of $\hat{x}$ and the length of y and of z.

20.

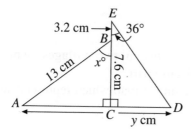

Find the value of x and of y, given that $\triangle ABC$ is congruent to $\triangle EDC$.

21.

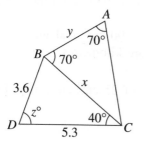

Given that $\triangle ABC$ and $\triangle CBD$ are congruent, find the values of x, y and z.

22. A model of a building is made using a scale $1 : 3\,000$.
   (a) The pinnacle of the building is 8 m long. What is the height of the pinnacle of the model?
   (b) The height of the model is 25 cm. What is the height of the building in metres?

23. A map is drawn to a scale of 1 : 40 000.
    (a) Two towns are 36 km apart. Calculate, in centimetres, their distance apart on the map.
    (b) On the map, a farm has an area of 45.5 cm². Calculate, in square kilometres, the actual area of the farm.

24. A model of a house is made to a scale of 5 to 800.
    (a) Express the scale in the form 1 : n.
    (b) Given that the volume of the roof is 80 640 m³, calculate the volume of the roof of the model.

25. A plot of land of area 144 km² is represented on the map by an area of 4 cm². This piece of land also contains a river 2 km long. Find the length of the river on the map.

26. The scale of a map is 1 : 50 000. Find
    (a) the actual distance, in metres, represented by 1 cm on the map,
    (b) the actual area, in square kilometres, represented by 5 cm² on the map.

27. A forest is represented by an area of 16 cm² on a map of scale 1 : 10 000. Find, in square centimetres, the area representing the same forest on a map of scale 1 : 2 500.

28. The scale of a map is 4 cm to 12 km.
    (a) Calculate the distance, in kilometres, between two villages, which are represented on the map by two dots 15 cm apart.
    (b) Calculate, in square centimetres, the area on the map which represents an area of 9 km² on the ground.

29. A map of a region is drawn on a scale of 1 : 50 000.
    (a) The length of a road is 15 km. Find the length of the line on the map which represents this road.
    (b) On the map, the area representing the forest is 200 cm². Calculate the actual area of the forest, giving your answer in square kilometres.

30. A forest of area 225 km² is represented by an area of 25 cm² on a map. Find the scale of the map in the form 1 : n.

31. A map is drawn to a scale of 1 : 50 000.
    (a) If two towns are 2 cm apart on the map, find their actual distance apart.
    (b) The actual area of town A is 3 km². Find the area of town A on the map.

32. If a plot of land of area 25 km² is represented on a map by 4 cm², find the scale of the map.

33. The diagram shows a scale drawing of a plot of land which contains a triangular playground 3 cm by 4 cm. Given that the actual area of the plot of land is 250 km² and the scale of the map is 1 : 300 000, find the area of the remaining land on the map.

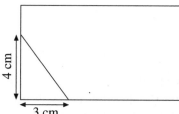

34. On a scale drawing, the length of a railway is 4 cm. The true length of the railway is 12 m. Find the scale in the form 1 : n.

35. The scale of a map is 2 cm to 1 km.
   (a) Express this ratio in the form 1 : n.
   (b) What is the distance between two towns which are 9 cm apart on the map?

36. The scale of a map is 1 : 250 000.
   (a) Find, in km, the length of a road which is 5 cm on the map.
   (b) Find the distance on the map between two towns which are 25 km away.

37. A length of 2 cm on a map represents a distance of 1 km.
   (a) What distance is represented by a length of 14 cm on the map?
   (b) What length on the map represents a distance of 600 m?

38. The plan of a house is drawn to a scale of 1 : 50.
   (a) Find the actual length, in metres, represented by 16 cm on the plan.
   (b) What length, in centimetres, on the plan represents an actual length of 12 m?

39. The R.F. of a map is $\dfrac{1}{20\,000}$. Find the actual distance, in kilometres, between two towns whose distance apart on the map is
   (a) 56 cm,
   (b) 32.8 cm,
   (c) 88 mm.

40. The R.F. of a map is $\dfrac{1}{500\,000}$. What distance, in centimetres, on the map will represent
   (a) 164 km,
   (b) 30 km,
   (c) 1 500 m?

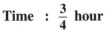
Time : $\dfrac{3}{4}$ hour

Marks : 40

ALL questions may be attempted.

Answers are to be written on the question paper in the spaces provided.

Omission of essential workings will result in loss of marks. No calculators are allowed.

This paper consists of 10 questions.

1. Evaluate the following:

   (a) $\left(2\dfrac{1}{3} + 1\dfrac{2}{9}\right) \times 2\dfrac{2}{5}$ [1]

   (b) $\{6 \times [108 \div (-17 + 8)] - 36\} + 12$ [2]

   (c) $12^2 - 2^3 + 7^2$ [1]

   Ans (a) _____

   (b) _____

   (c) _____

2. Given that $-3 \leqslant p \leqslant 4$ and $2 \leqslant q \leqslant 6$, find

   (a) the least possible value of $p - q$, [1]

   (b) the least possible value of pq. [1]

   Ans (a) _____

   (b) _____

3. **(a)** For each of the following figures, draw the lines of symmetry. [2]

(i)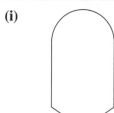

(ii)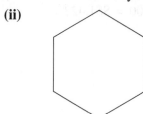

(b) State the order of rotational symmetry of each of the following figures below.
[2]

(i)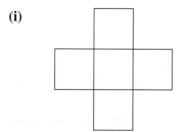

(ii)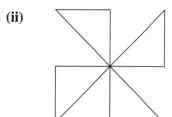

4. **(a)** For each of the following number sequences, fill in the missing terms.

(i) 2, _____, 5, _____, 12, 17, 23, 30. [2]

(ii) $\frac{2}{3}$, 1, $1\frac{2}{3}$, $2\frac{2}{3}$, 4, $5\frac{2}{3}$, _____, _____. [2]

Ans (i) _____

(ii) _____

(b) Arrange the following in descending order.

(i) 5, –2, 0, –4, 3 [2]

(ii) $-\frac{1}{2}$, $-\frac{3}{4}$, $-\frac{7}{8}$ [2]

Ans (i) _____

(ii) _____

5. **(a)** What is the amount of US\$ Mrs Lee gets for S\$5 680 if the conversion rate is US\$1.00 = S\$1.42? [2]

Ans _____

(b) Find x when $7 : x = 35 : 5$. [1]

Ans _____

6. Given that $x = 4$, $y = 3$ and $z = -2$, find the value of
(a) $7x + 5y$, [1]
(b) $3x^2 - 4y^2z$. [2]

Ans (a) _____

(b) _____

7. **(a)** Express \$21 as a percentage of \$60. [1]

Ans _____

(b) Calculate $28\frac{1}{2}\%$ of 40 m. [1]

Ans _____

(c) Susan obtained 78% in a Mathematics Assessment Test. The full marks was 250. How many marks did she get for her Mathematics Test? [2]

Ans _____

8. (a) Correct the following to the nearest whole number and then estimate the value of the expression correct to 1 significant figure.
$$\frac{59.89 \times 3.14}{15.16}$$ [2]

Ans _____

(b) Express 3.5 cm² in m². [2]

Ans _____

9. (a) A hollow cylinder standing on a horizontal circular base of diameter 20 cm contains water to a depth of 12 cm. Find the volume of water in terms of π. [2]

Ans _____

(b) Find x and y in the given diagram. [2]

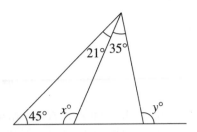

Ans $x =$ _____

$y =$ _____

10. (a) A factory worker reported for work at 08 45. He worked for $8\frac{1}{2}$ hours. At what time did he stop work? Give your answer in the 12-hour notation. [2]

Ans _____

(b) A clock gains 12 minutes 15 seconds in one week. How many days will it take to gain 1 hour and 45 minutes? [2]

Ans _____

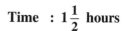

FINAL TERM ASSESSMENT PAPER 2

Time : $1\frac{1}{2}$ hours

Marks : 60

This paper consists of 2 sections.
Section A consists of **6 questions**.
Section B consists of **5 questions**.
Calculators may be used in this paper. If the degree of accuracy is not specified and if the answer is not exact, the answer should be given to 3 significant figures.

Section A (28 marks)
ALL *questions may be attempted.*

1. Evaluate the following, giving your answers correct to 4 significant figures.

   (a) $\dfrac{\sqrt{84.6} \times 0.6^3}{\sqrt[3]{0.014}}$ [2]

   (b) $\dfrac{(23 - 7.84)^2 - 8.79}{5 \times (3.7 + 4.1 - 2.8)^2}$ [2]

   Ans (a) _____

   (b) _____

2. Solve the following equations:
   (a) $8(4 - y) = 6(3 - y)$ [2]
   (b) $\dfrac{3x - 1}{5} - \dfrac{x + 5}{3} = 4$ [2]

   Ans (a) _____

   (b) _____

3. (a) A clumsy painter is engaged to paint an office. He spills $\frac{1}{10}$ of every can of paint he opens. 64.8 litres of paint are required to paint the office. If each can contains 4.8 litres of paint, calculate how many cans of paint are required. [3]

Ans _____

(b) Fifty-one men, working 8 hours a day, are needed to finish a project. If 3 men are unable to report for work, how long should the rest work a day to finish the project on time? [4]

Ans _____

4. Construct $\triangle ABC$ given that AB = 4 cm, BC = 5.5 cm and CA = 7 cm. Construct the bisector of angle ACB. The bisector of angle ACB cuts AB at P. Measure and write down the length of AP. [5]

Ans _____

5. (a) The sum of the interior angles of a polygon of n sides is 10 right angles. Find n. [2]

Ans _____

(b) The interior angles of a quadrilateral are in the ratio 1 : 2 : 3 : 4. What is the value of the largest exterior angle? [2]

Ans _____

6. (a) In the diagram, *ABCD* is similar to *PQRS*. Calculate the value of *x* and of *y*.

[2]

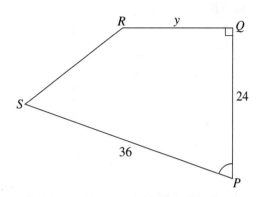

Ans x _____

y _____

(b) In the diagram, ABC is a right-angled triangle with $A\hat{B}C = 90°$. DE is parallel to AB.

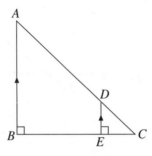

(i) Name a triangle which is similar to $\triangle ABC$. [1]

(ii) Given that $AC = 21$ cm and $CD = 6$ cm, find the length of DE when $AB = 14$ cm. [1]

Ans (i) _____

(ii) _____

Section B (32 marks)
Answer any **FOUR** *questions.*

1. Consider the following sequence:

$$2 + 6 \qquad\qquad = 8 \ = 2 \times 2^2$$
$$2 + 6 + 10 \qquad = 18 = 2 \times 3^2$$
$$2 + 6 + 10 + 14 = 32 = 2 \times 4^2$$

(a) Write down, in the given space below, the fifth line of the sequence. [1]

_____

(b) Find the sum of $2 + 6 + 10 + 14 + ... + 38$. [1]

_____

(c) A given line of the sequence is as follows:
$$2 + 6 + 10 + 14 + ... + q = 512 = 2 \times p^2$$
Find the value of p and of q. [4]

Ans p = _____

q = _____

(d) Write down a formula, in terms of n, for the sum of the nth line of the sequence. [2]

Ans _____

2. (a) In a game of dice, $5\frac{1}{2}$ points is scored when an even number is thrown and $3\frac{1}{4}$ points is lost when an odd number is thrown.

(i) How many points do I score if I throw a three, 4 sixes, a five and 3 twos? [2]

(ii) How many odd numbers and how many even numbers should there be so that my final score is 10 if I throw the dice 5 times? [4]

Ans (i) _____

(ii) _____

(b) The interest on a man's investment increases from $8\frac{3}{4}\%$ to $11\frac{1}{4}\%$ per annum. Find the value of his investment if his annual income from it increases by $75. [2]

Ans _____

3. A path 1 m wide is constructed round a rectangular lawn. The path is made of slab of side 0.5 m each. Calculate
- **(a)** the number of concrete slabs required for the path, [4]
- **(b)** the volume of one concrete slab, in cubic metres, given that the square slab is 5 cm thick (Give your answer to 3 decimal places), [2]
- **(c)** the total volume of concrete, in cubic metres, used in making the path, [1]
- **(d)** the cost of laying the path if one cubic metre of concrete costs $555. [1]

11 m

8 m

Ans (a) _____

(b) _____

(c) _____

(d) _____

4. **(a)** Find the length of *DE* if *DA* = 24 cm, *DC* = 8 cm and *DF* = 6 cm. [3]

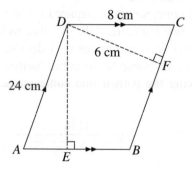

(b) Find the values of x and y for the following diagrams:

(i)

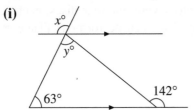

(ii)

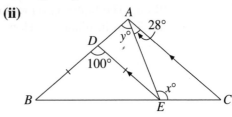

[2]   [3]

Ans (i) _____

(ii) _____

5. (a) Butter in the shape of a solid cylinder has a diameter of 6 cm and a length of 10 cm. The butter is remoulded into several circular discs, each 0.8 cm thick and 3 cm in diameter. How many discs can be formed? (Take π = 3.142) [4]

Ans _____

(b) A man walking at 4.8 km/h takes 1 hour 45 minutes to complete a journey. How much time does he save if he cycles instead at a speed of 12 km/h? Give your answer in hours and minutes, correct to the nearest minute. [4]

Ans _____

ANSWERS

Chapter 1

1. (a) 441 **(b)** 14 **2.** 129 **3.** 17
4. (a) 240 **(b)** 45 **(c)** 84 **(d)** 41 **(e)** 635
5. (a) 20 603 **(b)** twenty four thousand and sixty five
6. (a) 1, 2, 3, 6, 9, 18 **(b)** 1, 2, 3, 5, 6, 10, 15, 30
 (c) 1, 2, 3, 4, 6, 8, 12, 16, 24, 48 **(d)** 1, 2, 3, 4, 6, 8, 9, 12, 18, 24, 36, 72
7. (a) $2^4 \times 3^2 \times 5 \times 7$ **(b)** 7
8. (a) 23, 37; 851 **(b)** 9, 16, 49; 74
9. (a) 2, 3, 5, 41 **(b)** 51
10. (a) $2^2 \times 3^2 \times 11 \times 19$ **(b)** 40
11. (a) $2^4 \times 3^2 \times 11$ **(b)** 11 **12.** $2^3 \times 3^2 \times 5^3$
13. (a) 2×7 **(b)** 2×13 **(c)** 2^5 **(d)** $3^2 \times 5$ **(e)** $2^3 \times 7$
 (f) $2^2 \times 17$ **(g)** 2×37 **(h)** $2^3 \times 17$ **(i)** $2^3 \times 5^2$ **(j)** 5×73
14. (a) 23 **(b)** 43 **(c)** 67 **(d)** 247
15. (a) 8 **(b)** 151, 157, 163, 167
16. (a) $3^2 \times 2^5$ **(b)** $29 \times 5 \times 3$ **17.** (a) 42 **(b)** 48
18. (a) 15 **(b)** $3ac$ **19.** (a) 63 **(b)** 169
20. (a) 432 **(b)** $72p^3qr^3$
21. (a) 136 **(b)** 18 **(c)** 200 **(d)** 144 **(e)** 45
22. $25xyz^3$; $125x^2y^3z^5$ **23.** $x = 2, y = 2, z = 2$

Chapter 2

1. $1\frac{15}{16}$ **2.** $\frac{4}{15}, \frac{5}{8}, \frac{11}{12}$ **3.** $-8\frac{2}{3}$ **4.** $\frac{41}{120}$ **5.** $\frac{3}{2}$

6. (a) $\frac{7}{8}$ **(b)** 33 **(c)** 46 **(d)** $\frac{3}{10}$

7. (a) 87.05 **(b)** 37.89 **8.** (a) 100.48 **(b)** 3.5

9. (a) 0.126 **(b)** 30 **10.** (a) $10\frac{3}{4}$ **(b)** 0.72 **(c)** 7.04

11. (a) (i) 58 (ii) 58.2 (iii) 58.235
 (b) (i) 40 (ii) 39.6 (iii) 39.593
 (c) (i) 64 (ii) 63.7 (iii) 63.725
 (d) (i) 88 (ii) 88.3 (iii) 88.329
12. 156.64 **13.** $35.46 **14.** (a) 4.33 **(b)** 0.045 6
15. 9.09 l **16.** (a) −0.56 **(b)** 26.37 **17.** 69
18. 28.26; 4.790 **19.** 64.1 **20.** (a) 0.005 38 **(b)** 56.2 **(c)** 190
21. 0.080 4 **22.** 2.46 **23.** (a) 14.8 **(b)** 5.79

24. (a) 2.875 **(b)** 15 680 **25.** (a) $\frac{25}{63}$ **(b)** $\frac{5}{3}$

26. (a) 3 **(b)** 6 **27.** (a) 2 **(b)** 18
28. (a) 0.05 **(b)** 4 **29.** (a) 200 **(b)** 200 **(c)** 300
30. 16 **31.** (a) 300 **(b)** 30 **(c)** 3.8

Test Paper 1

1. (a) 32   (b) 50.4   2. (a) 22.28   (b) $\dfrac{13}{15}$

3. (a) 5 300   (b) 0.117   4. (a) 35   (b) 5.7

5. (a) $\dfrac{2}{5}$, 0.45, $\dfrac{2}{3}$, 0.95   (b) 0.3, $\dfrac{3}{7}$, 0.5, $\dfrac{3}{5}$

    (c) $\dfrac{3}{8}$, $\dfrac{4}{9}$, $\dfrac{9}{20}$, $\dfrac{7}{13}$ (d) $\dfrac{1}{5}$, 0.2$\dot{4}$, 0.24$\dot{5}$, 0.25

6. (a) 18, 2 700   (b) 35, 6 300   (c) 13, 130   (d) 11, 5 082
7. (a) 70   (b) 30

8. (a) $2\dfrac{2}{9}$ (b) $\dfrac{17}{23}$ (c) $\dfrac{2}{3}$ (d) 0.135

Chapter 3

1. (a) 0.010 03 kg   (b) 1 kg 10 g   (c) 100 001 g
    (d) 7 400m   (e) 101 cm   (f) 0.032 m
    (g) 6 m 1 cm   (h) 780 s   (i) 143 min
    (j) 5 min 1 s   (k) 8 120 s
2. 137 min   3. 82 cm   4. $520.55   5. $67.26
6. 18 h 5 min   7. $25.14   8. $4.20   9. $13.30

10. $\dfrac{63}{160}$ 11. $72   12. 534   13. $34\dfrac{1}{7}$ kg

14. (a) $7.10   (b) $10.20   15. $\dfrac{4}{15}$ 16. $67.83, 23

17. (a) $5.25   (b) 5   18. (a) 210   (b) 103   (c) 1 720

19. 100   20. $14.20   21. $2\dfrac{1}{18}$ m   22. 03 20 h   23. 11.21 h

24. (a) 1.347 5 m (b) 38 kg   25. –7   26. $27.08   27. $72.90
28. (a) 16   (b) $7.50   29. (a) 8 h 38 min   (b) 1 h 55 min
30. $18   31. 12th of the month
32. (a) $163   (b) 17.351 5   33. (a) 5.5 l (b) $30.36
34. (a) 4 h 30 min, 7 h 25 min   (b) 4 h 40 min
35. (a) 34   (b) $130   36. (a) 1 920 km   (b) $14 580
37. 250   38. (a) $3   (b) $6   (c) $183   (d) $421.55
39. (a) $4   (b) $153   (c) 67 h   40. (a) $71.60 (b) 256 km
41. (a) $183.60   (b) 325 km   42. (a) $737.50   (b) $46 000
43. (a) $101   (b) $1 308

Chapter 4

1. 31   2. 34
3. (a) 15, 18, 21, 24 (b) –2, 4, 6, 8   (c) –10, –5, 5, 15
4. (a) –153   (b) –116   (c) –359   (d) –115
    (e) 527   (f) –378
5. (a) –901   (b) –377   (c) 1 746   (d) 0
6. (a) 48   (b) 400   (c) 1 344   (d) 225
7. (a) 20.62   (b) 65.19   8. 22.415   9. 1

10. 280   **11.** 121

12. (a) -13 (b) 21   (c) 9   (d) -15

13. (a) $7^2 \times 2^6$ (b) 56

14. (a) 8   (b) -80 (c) -29 (d) -19 (e) 15

15. (a) $\dfrac{4}{5}$ (b) 0.9   (c) $2\dfrac{2}{3}$ **16.** (a) $\dfrac{7}{50}$ (b) $-3\dfrac{1}{12}$

17. (a) $\dfrac{6}{5}$ (b) 68.70   **18.** (a) $1\dfrac{13}{21}$ (b) $\dfrac{1}{20}$

19. (a) $\dfrac{1}{81}$ (b) 11   (c) $\dfrac{1}{6}$ (d) $\dfrac{1}{27}$ (e) 4

20. (a) $1\dfrac{3}{5}$ (b) $\dfrac{7}{128}$ **21.** 0.297 5   **22.** $20\dfrac{23}{24}$

23. (a) 48   (b) $\dfrac{41}{15}$ (c) 0.025

24. (a) -7.14 (b) -16.0 **25.** 0.018 1   **26.** (a) 20   (b) $\dfrac{1}{6}$

27. $\dfrac{5}{14}$ **28.** (a) 384   (b) 100   **29.** 372

30. (a) 1 175   (b) 49   **31.** (a) -4.2 (b) 4   **32.** 31

33. (a) -196 (b) -5.694 **34.** $-21\dfrac{1}{8}$ **35.** 3.3

36. (a) 0.340 8   (b) 13.89   **37.** 9   **38.** $\dfrac{7}{4}$

39. (a) $5\dfrac{3}{8}$ (b) -1.682 **40.** (a) -47 (b) -24

41. (a) $15\dfrac{3}{7}$ (b) 7.64   **42.** $-\dfrac{1}{3}$

43. (a) -23.25 (b) 4   **44.** (a) 14.8   (b) 0.041 4

Test Paper 2

1. (a) 415 g   (b) 129.6   **2.** (a) 90   (b) $\dfrac{8}{3}$

3. 0.151 7   **4.** (a) 1.414   (b) $1\dfrac{1}{2}$ (c) $2\dfrac{3}{38}$ **5.** 56

6. (a) \$2.25   (b) 11   **7.** (a) 06 45   (b) \$9   (c) \$367.50

8. (a) (i) 46   (ii) 180 cm   (b) \$11 250

Chapter 5

1. (a) $m + 10$ (b) $2n$ (c) $pq - 5$

2. $\dfrac{50}{a}$ **3.** $0.3x + 0.16y$ **4.** $45 - w - x$

5. (a) $x + 3$ (b) $90x + 150$ **6.** $\dfrac{(4x + 7)(2x - 1)}{2}$

7. (a) $h + k + 2p$ (b) $20h + 15k + 50p$ **8.** $2(2h + 2k - 1)$

9. (a) $4\dfrac{41}{45}$ (b) $3\dfrac{14}{25}$ **10.** (a) $-\dfrac{5}{6}$ (b) 3

11. (a) -6 **(b)** 143 **12.** $-\dfrac{21}{16}$

13. (a) 21 **(b)** -222 **14. (a)** 47 **(b)** 21
15. (a) 18 **(b)** -1 **(c)** 9
16. (a) 13 **(b)** 104 **17. (a)** 36 **(b)** 125
18. (a) -2 **(b)** 3 **(c)** -12 **19.** 4
20. (a) 17 **(b)** 98 **(c)** -91
21. (a) 0 **(b)** -10 **(c)** 7

22. (a) $17\dfrac{3}{4}$ **(b)** $7\dfrac{1}{4}$ **(c)** $251\dfrac{1}{4}$

  (d) $-3\dfrac{15}{16}$ **(e)** $10\dfrac{1}{2}$ **(f)** $19\dfrac{1}{2}$

23. (a) $35\ wx$ **(b)** $-24\ wx$ **(c)** $42\ mn^2$ **(d)** $-36p^3q^2$
  (e) $-135c^2$ **(f)** $92a^2$

24. (a) $14a$ **(b)** $\dfrac{7}{2}x$ **(c)** $-\dfrac{2}{3q}$ **(d)** $\dfrac{13d}{b}$

  (e) $\dfrac{s}{5p}$ **(f)** $\dfrac{72}{b}$

25. (a) $4b-5a$ **(b)** $-3a-8b$ **(c)** $-\dfrac{1}{6}x+\dfrac{5}{9}y$ **26.** $24y-15x$

27. (a) $4a-3b$ **(b)** $3a-2$ **28.** $-\dfrac{29}{6}a-21$

29. (a) $\dfrac{x-4}{15}$ **(b)** $\dfrac{3}{2}y-\dfrac{21}{20}x$ **30.** $4x^2-2x-1$

31. (a) $-12x-9$ **(b)** $2x^2+4x+y$ **32. (a)** $\dfrac{7}{30}a-\dfrac{31}{30}b$ **(b)** $24a+24c$

33. (a) $9t-23$ **(b)** $\dfrac{17-2x}{15}$
34. (a) $8x-3y$ **(b)** $-2(t+8)$ **(c)** $16y-29$ **(d)** $5b-4a$
  (e) $3(p^2-17p+5)$ **(f)** x **(g)** $3(2a-b)$
35. (a) $a(29a+1)$ **(b)** $18p+24q+13r-p^2$
  (c) $7w^2+12p^2+10w$ **(d)** $3ab-6ac+4bc$
  (e) $-2(hj+4kh+kj)$ **(f)** $w(6yx^2+3wy-5x-4)$

36. (a) $9a-2$ **(b)** $\dfrac{5p+9}{8}$ **(c)** $\dfrac{33x^2-8}{7}$

  (d) $\dfrac{31x+6}{60}$ **(e)** $\dfrac{13p+3q}{16}$ **(f)** $\dfrac{5w-6x+60}{15}$

37. (a) $69x-9y$ **(b)** $-14s-14r$

Chapter 6

1. 6 **2.** 20 **3.** $\dfrac{5}{11}$ **4.** 10 **5.** ±6

6. $\pm\dfrac{4}{9}$ **7.** ±9 **8.** 2 **9.** -12 **10.** ±3

11. $-\dfrac{1}{20}$ **12.** ±9 **13.** -7

14. (a) -3 **(b)** 80 **(c)** $-\dfrac{1}{14}$ **(d)** $\dfrac{8}{11}$ **(e)** 9 **(f)** $\dfrac{23}{7}$

15. (a) 1   (b) 33   (c) $\dfrac{3}{7}$ (d) 90   (e) −2   (f) $\dfrac{9}{5}$

16. (a) 0.95   (b) 2.22   (c) −2.15   (d) 37.25   (e) 66.67   (f) 0.83

17. (a) 16   (b) 8   **18.** 14.83   **19.** 45

20. (a) 12   (b) 768   **21.** (a) 104   (b) 121.11   **22.** 209.52

23. 1.26   **24.** 18   **25.** 36   **26.** 1 088   **27.** 140p cents

28. (a) \$4x (b) \$3 400   (c) \$9 000   **29.** \$4.20

30. (a) $15x + (16 - x)20 = 300$, 4   (b) no change

31. \$39.90   **32.** 33   **33.** 2

34. (a) 14.625 cm   (b) 287.5 cm^2 **35.** 21, 23

36. (a) 18   (b) \$80   **37.** (a) $\dfrac{150}{x}$ (b) $\dfrac{150}{x} + 0.5$, 50

38. 70 20¢ stamps, 30 15¢ stamps   **39.** $3.5x + 2x(9.5) = 135$, $x = 6$, 18

40. (a) $4x - 1$ (b) $x - 3$

41. (a) 40   (b) (i) $(120 + x)$ cents   (ii) $\dfrac{3\,600}{120 + x}$

     (c) $\dfrac{3\,600}{120 + x}(120 + 2x) = 3\,825$; 8

42. (a) \$134   (b) 400   (c) $M = 65 + \dfrac{21n}{100}$ (d) 250

Test Paper 3

1. (a) $\dfrac{25}{36}$ (b) $-13\dfrac{3}{80}$ **2.** (a) $\dfrac{11x + 43}{12}$ (b) $\dfrac{28y - 8}{5}$

3. (a) 2   (b) −0.057   (c) −3   (d) $-\dfrac{13}{8}$

4. (a) 60   (b) 6   **5.** 27, 4

6. (a) 4.5x (b) $\dfrac{x}{200}$ (c) $\dfrac{x}{200} \times 135 = 810$; $x = 1\,200$

Chapter 7

1. 17.4 km/h   **2.** 7.5 km/h   **3.** 135 km

4. (a) 3 h 44 min   (b) $17\dfrac{1}{3}$ km/h

5. (a) 27 km   (b) 8 km/h   (c) $14\dfrac{2}{3}$ km/h

6. 7 km/h   **7.** 28.8 km/h

8. (a) 1 508   (b) 33 km/h   **9.** (a) $1\dfrac{9}{10}$ h   (b) 39 min

10. (a) 820.31 km   (b) 41.02 cm   **11.** (a) 17 15   (b) 10.9 km/h

12. 52 min

13. (a) 1 : 6   (b) 5 : 3   (c) 300 : 23   (d) 1 : 250

14. (a) 35   (b) $\dfrac{15}{2}$ (c) $\dfrac{9}{10}$ **15.** 16 cm

16. 21 cm   **17.** (a) \$122.50 (b) 10   **18.** \$600

19. (a) \$500   (b) \$1 250   **20.** (a) 8 cm by 6 cm   (b) 48 cm^2

21. 60°   **22.** \$200, \$400, \$1 000

23. (a) 230   (b) \$240

24. (a) 33.3% (b) (i) 80% (ii) $40
25. (a) $687.50 (b) $790.63 26. 107.812 5 m^2; 143.75%
27. (a) $920 (b) $1 656
28. (a) 50.4 kg; 42 kg (b) 210 pounds 29. (a) 55% (b) 675

30. (a) 0.55 (b) $\dfrac{11}{20}$ 31. (a) 38% (b) 144

32. 2 200 33. 21 34. 3 h 36 min 35. 4

36. (a) 9 cm (b) 1 130.4 cm^2 37. 35

38. (a) $855 (b) 26 h 39. 4
40. (a) $40.80 (b) $2.80 41. 352 km

Mid-Term Assessment Paper 1
1. (a) 100 (b) 14 2. (a) −67 (b) −21

3. (a) $-\dfrac{1}{14}$ (b) $1\dfrac{1}{3}$ 4. (a) 10 (b) 1.342

5. (a) 5, 105 (b) 16, 192 6. (a) $2w - 7v$ (b) $\dfrac{21b - 10a}{4}$

7. (a) $-22\dfrac{1}{5}$ (b) −9 8. (a) −2 (b) −3
9. 10 10. (a) 5 h (b) 85 km/h

11. (a) $62\dfrac{1}{2}\%$ (b) 75 kg 12. (a) 26 (b) $4.60

Mid-Term Assessment Paper 2
Section A
1. (a) (i) −9 780 (ii) 0.008 19 (b) (i) 145 (ii) 75
2. $16.88 3. 49 4. $1.12; $1.05
5. (a) 83.87% (b) 16.13% 6. (a) 87° (b) 168°

Section B
1. (a) (i) 16.99 (ii) 38.14 (b) (i) 64 (ii) 32

2. (a) (i) $9(2x - y)$ (ii) $\dfrac{13a + 11b}{9}$ (b) (i) $-\dfrac{20}{31}$ (ii) $-\dfrac{37}{7}$

   (c) Lin: 12, Susan: 16, Janet: 34

3. (a) $23.91 (b) (i) $14\dfrac{3}{10}$ m (ii) $6\dfrac{1}{2}$ m (iii) $7\dfrac{4}{5}$

4. (a) 75 cm (b) (i) $980; $644 (ii) $196
5. (a) (i) 27 kg 632 g (ii) 20.83 m/s
   (b) 22 (c) (i) 96.8 km (ii) 1.98 h (1 h 59 min)

Chapter 8
1. 25% 2. 30% 3. (a) $5 500 (b) $3 500; 57.1%
4. (a) £89.68 (b) $3 344.06 5. (a) $500 (b) $690
6. $679.80 7. (a) 12.2% (b) 26.7%
8. (a) $6.72 (b) $437.50 9. $455; $600 10. $160
11. 6 375 yen; £1 214.29 12. (a) $45 760 (b) $2 392

13. $37.81 **14.** $1 054 **15.** $20\frac{5}{6}\%$; $118.75

16. (a) $1 500 **(b)** 15%

17. I would advise him to buy the television set because the cost of buying is $1 350 while the cost of renting is $1 542.

18. (a) $42.50 **(b)** $250 **19.** $100 **20.** $960

21. (a) $5 444 **(b)** $5 040.74 **22.** $88.97

23. (a) $73.41 **(b)** $60.30 **24.** $23.80

25. (a) $81 **(b)** 7 years **26. (a)** $24.40 **(b)** $12.295 **(c)** $36.36

27. (a) $4 160.00 **(b)** £168.75

28. (a) $9 400 000 **(b)** 64.9% **(c)** $21 900 000

29. 20 **30. (a)** 318 francs **(b)** £7.50

31. (a) $1 200 **(b)** $16 800

32. (a) $64 000 **(b)** 10% **(c)** $800 **(d)** $100 000

Chapter 9

1. (a) 50° **(b)** 22° **(c)** 17° **(d)** 15° **(e)** 13 **(f)** 54°

2. (a) $x = 20°, y = 120°$ **(b)** $x = 48°, y = 132°$ **(c)** $x = 22.5°, y = 90°$
   (d) $x = 16°, y = 85°$ **(e)** $x = 21°, y = 98°$

3. 12° **4.** 25° **5.** 30°

6. (a) $x = 38°, y = 34°, z = 74°$ **(b)** $x = 136°, y = 22°$
   (c) $x = 18°$ **(d)** $x = 15.5°, y = 87°$
   (e) $x = 77°, y = 103°$ **(f)** $x = 60°, y = 60°, z = 45°$

7. (a) $x = 83°$ **(b)** $x = 80°$ **(c)** $x = 262°$ **(d)** $x = 128°$
   (e) $x = 60°$ **(f)** $x = 94°$ **(g)** $x = 88°$ **(h)** $x = 18°$
   (i) $x = 130°$ **(j)** $x = 28°$

8. 37° **9.** 22.5° **10.** $a = 100°, b = 56°$

11. (a) 70° **(b)** 83°

12. 15° **13.** $x = 31.5°, y = 91.5°$

14. $x = 120°, y = 60°$ **15.** $x = 65, y = 250$

16. (a) $x = 120, y = 52$ **(b)** $x = 30, y = 136$
   (c) $x = 39, y = 46$ **(d)** $x = 127, y = 77$

17.  **18.**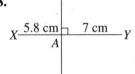

X—5.8 cm—A—7 cm—Y

19.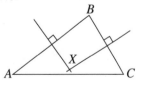

Test Paper 4

1. (a) 13.86% **(b)** $357.50

2. (a) $57.63 **(b) (i)** $62.90 **(ii)** 9.14%

3. (a) 340 dollars **(b)** £450

4. (a) (i) $23.75 **(ii)** $255 **(iii)** $1 128.75
   (b) $205.35 **(c) (i)** $186 **(ii)** $1 507.35

5. **(a)** \$53.25   **(b)** 142 kW/h   **6.** 61°

7. $x = 26°$, $W\hat{X}Y = 78°$

8. **(a)** **(i)** $x = 20°$, $y = 80°$ **(ii)** $x = 118°$, $y = 59°$

    (b)

Chapter 10

1. **(a)** $x = 25°$ **(b)** $x = 30.5°$, $y = 61°$ **(c)** $x = 12\frac{6}{7}°$

    (d) $x = 20°$, $y = 30°$, $z = 60°$ **(e)** $x = 29.7$

2. 30°   **3.** 131°   **4.** 8°   **5.** 135°   **6.** 43°

7. 60°   **8.** $x = 21°$ **9.** $x = 65°$, $y = 50°$

10. $x = 86°$, $y = 124°$ **11.** $x = 30°$, $y = 24°$ **12.** 36°

13. **(a)** $x = 42°$ **(b)** $x = 42°$, $y = 56°$, $z = 82°$

     (c) $x = 115°$, $y = 138°$ **(d)** $x = 15°$, $y = 15°$

14. **(a)** isosceles triangle   **(b)** 22.5°

15. $\hat{R} = 33°$ **16.**

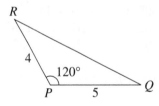

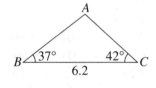

17. $AC = 5.5$ cm   **18.**

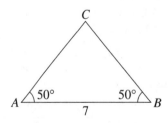

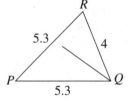

19. **(a)** 51°   **(b)** 24°

20.   **21.**

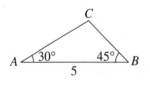

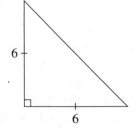

22.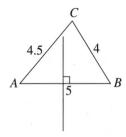

23.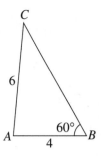

24. $x = 65°$, $y = 115°$

25. 11

26. (a) $x = 86°$, $y = 34°$, $z = 34°$ (b) $x = 50°$, $y = 58°$, $z = 32°$

27. (a) $x = 122°$, $y = 54°$, $z = 24°$ (b) $x = 114°$, $y = 72°$, $z = 108°$

28. 74°   **29.** $x = 55°$, $y = 109°$ **30.** $x = 15°$, $y = 100°$

31. (a) 160°   (b) 24   **32.** (a) 18°   (b) 140°

33. 3   **34.** (a) 8   (b) 11.25°   **35.** 36°

36. (a) 5   (b) 53.5°   **37.** 36

38. (a) 30°   (b) 120°

39.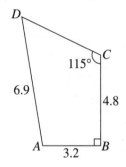

40.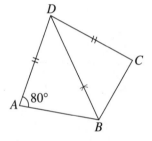

41. (a) 54°   (b) 12

42.

43.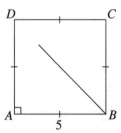

44.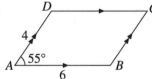

45. 9.2 cm

46. $AC = 7.7$ cm
$BD = 10.2$ cm

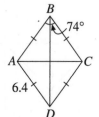

147

Chapter 11

1. (a) 0   (b) 1   (c) 8

2.

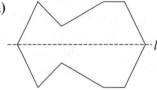

3.

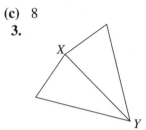

4. (a)

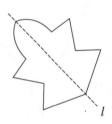

(b)

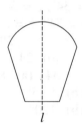

(c)

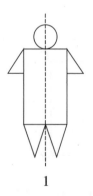

(d)

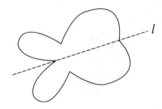

5. (a)

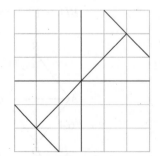

1

(b)

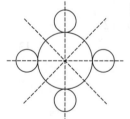

4

(c)

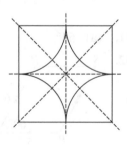

4

6.

148

7. (a) 1   **(b)** ∞   **(c)** 6   **8.**

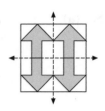

9. (a) kite   **(b)** rectangle   **(c)** square
10. (a) 4   **(b)** 3   **(c)** 1
11. (a) 2   **(b)** 2   **(c)** 2
12. (a) 2   **(b)** 3   **(c)** 4
13.

14.

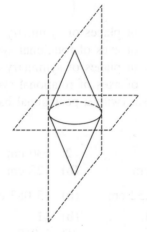

15. (a) 3   **(b)** 5   **(c)** 4
16. (a) 4; 1   **(b)** ∞; 1
17. (a) 4   **(b)** ∞   **(c)** 1
18. (a) cylinder   **(b)** sphere   **(c)** cuboid   **(d)** cone
19. (a)   **(b)**

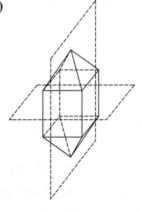

Test Paper 5
1. (a) $x = 62°, y = 30°$ **(b)** $x = 62°, y = 56°, z = 118°$
    (c) $x = 59°, y = 73.5°$ **(d)** $x = 64°, y = 44°, z = 26°$
2. (a) $x = 28°, y = 56°, z = 112°$ **(b)** $x = 30°, y = 30°, z = 120°$
3. (a) 30   **(b)** 78°   **(c)** 60°
4.

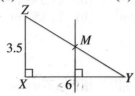

$YM = 3.4$

5. (a)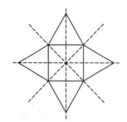

(b)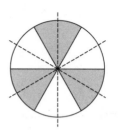

No. of lines of symmetry = 4
Order of rotational symmetry = 4

No. of lines of symmetry = 3
Order of rotational symmetry = 3

6. (a)

(b)

(c)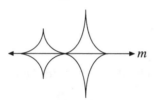

(d)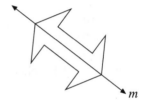

7. (a) No. of planes of symmetry = 7
No. of axes of rotational symmetry = 7
(b) No. of planes of symmetry = infinitely many
No. of axes of rotational symmetry = 1
8. right prism (with a pentagonal base)

Chapter 12
1. 360 cm   **2.** 630 cm   **3.** 16 cm
4. (a) 32 cm   **(b)** 128 cm   **5.** 13 cm   **6.** 9.5 cm
7. (a) 188.52 cm   **(b)** 15 082 cm   **8.** $121\frac{1}{5}$ cm   **9.** 2 612.48
10. (a) 54.3   **(b)** 41   **(c)** 30   **(d)** 61.1
    (e) 60   **(f)** 1 040   **(g)** 57   **(h)** 13.36
11. (a) 104.5   **(b)** 19.63   **(c)** 48   **(d)** 116.1
12. (a) 3.532 5 km^2 **(b)** 10.71 km
13. (a) 2 800 m^2 **(b)** 156 m^2 **(c)** 96 m^2 **14.** 5.2 cm
15. (a) 18.75 cm^2 **(b)** 4.69 cm   **16. (a)** 12 cm^2 **(b)** 6 cm^2
17. (a) 21 cm   **(b)** 13 cm^2 **18. (a)** 7.5 cm^2 **(b)** 47.5 cm^2
19. (a) 20 + 6π **(b)** 36π – 30   **20. (a)** 7.07 cm^2 **(b)** 24.85 cm^2
21. (a) 3.46 m^2 **(b)** 10.39 m^2

Chapter 13
1. 0.226 m   **2.** 75 861 cm^3 **3. (a)** 187.2 m^3 **(b)** 160.92 m^2

4. (b) 4 m **5.** 514 cm^2; 770 cm^3 **6.** 235.5 m^3
7. (a) 160 cm^3 **(b)** 204 cm^2 **8. (a)** 153.86 cm^2 **(b)** 2 000 cm^2
9. (a) $2x^2 + 4xy$ **(b)** 4.47
10. (a) 736 **(b) (i)** 960 **(ii)** 120 **11.** 3
12. (a) 22 **(b)** 44 **13.** 7 622 **14.** 78 **15.** 1 456.96
16. (a) 260; 292 **(b)** 390; 382 **(c)** 216; 264
  (d) 109.96; 251.33 **(e)** 144; 204 **(f)** 56; 128
17. (a) 29 cm by 21 cm by 11 cm **(b)** 7 920 cm^3
  (c) 6 699 cm^3 **(d)** 1 221 cm^3 **(e)** 1.465 2 g
18. 2.25 cm **19.** 0.314 **20.** 19.31 g/cm^3 **21.** 26.231 cm^3
22. 5 002 **23.** 104 **24.** 8 960 cm^3 **25.** 117.56 cm^3
26. 88 cm^2 **27.** 280 m^2

Test Paper 6

1. (a) 4.4 cm^2 **(b)** 22.848 cm **2. (a)** 6 cm **(b)** 4 cm
3. (a) 252 cm^2, 61.87 cm **(b)** 57.75 cm^2, 40 cm
4. 3 520 m **5.** 160.2 cm^2 **6. (a)** \$4.875 **(b)** 1.416 m **(c)** 84 mm
7. (a) 703.81 **(b)** 4 222.86 g **8. (a)** 2 000 cm^3 **(b)** 36

Chapter 14

1. $a = \dfrac{16}{3}$, $b = \dfrac{9}{2}$ **2.** $BC = 9.6$ cm, $DF = 25$ cm

3. 3 **4.** $4\dfrac{4}{9}$ **5.** $XY = 3.4$ cm, $YZ = 4.1$ cm, $B\hat{A}C = 44°$

6. (a) $3 : 5$ **(b)** $4\dfrac{1}{6}$ cm **7.** 14 cm **8. (a)** 15 **(b)** $2 : 5$

9. $\dfrac{5}{2}$ **10. (a)** $CD = 24$ km, $AE = 18$ km **(b)** 342 km^2

11. $5\dfrac{1}{3}$ **12. (a)** $6\dfrac{2}{3}$ cm **(b)** 8 cm

13. (a) 5 **(b)** $2 : 7$ **14. (a)** $3 : 7$ **(b)** $4 : 7$

15. (a) $\triangle ABE$ and $\triangle DBC$ **(b)** $BC = 22.5$ cm; $B\hat{C}D = 50°$
16. (a) 1.67 cm **(b)** $1 : 3$
17. (a) & (g); (b) & (f); (c) & (h); (d) & (i); (e) & (j)
18. $x = 54°$, $y = 20$ **19.** $\hat{x} = 24°$, $y = 6.5$, $z = 3.5$
20. $x = 54°$, $y = 18.4$ cm **21.** $x = 5.3$, $y = 3.6$, $z = 70°$
22. (a) 0.27 cm **(b)** 750 m **23. (a)** 90 cm **(b)** 7.28 km^2
24. (a) $1 : 160$ **(b)** 19 687.5 cm^3 **25.** $\dfrac{1}{3}$ cm
26. (a) 500 m **(b)** 1.25 km^2 **27.** 256 cm^2
28. (a) 45 km **(b)** 1 cm^2 **29. (a)** 30 cm **(b)** 50 km^2
30. $1 : 300\,000$ **31. (a)** 1 km **(b)** 12 cm^2
32. $1 : 250\,000$ **33.** $21\dfrac{7}{9}$ cm^2 **34.** $1 : 300$
35. (a) $1 : 50\,000$ **(b)** 4.5 km **36. (a)** 12.5 km **(b)** 10 cm
37. (a) 7 km **(b)** 1.2 cm **38. (a)** 8 m **(b)** 24 cm
39. (a) 11.2 km **(b)** 6.56 km **(c)** 1.76 km
40. (a) 32.8 cm **(b)** 6 cm **(c)** 0.3 cm

Final Term Assessment Paper 1

1. (a) $8\frac{8}{15}$ (b) -96 (c) 185 2. (a) -9 (b) -18

3. (a) (i)

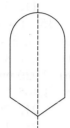

(ii)

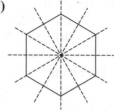

   (b) (i) 4   (ii) 4

4. (a) (i) 3, 8   (ii) $7\frac{2}{3}$, 10

   (b) (i) 5, 3, 0, -2, -4 (ii) $-\frac{1}{2}$, $-\frac{3}{4}$, $-\frac{7}{8}$

5. (a) US$4 000   (b) 1   6. (a) 43   (b) 120
7. (a) 35%   (b) 11.4 m   (c) 195
8. (a) 12   (b) 0.000 35
9. (a) $1\,200\pi$ (b) $x = 114°$, $y = 101°$
10. (a) 5.15 p.m.   (b) 60 days

Final Term Assessment Paper 2

Section A

1. (a) 8.243   (b) 1.768   2. (a) 7   (b) 22

3. (a) 15   (b) $8\frac{1}{2}$ h   4. $AP = 2.2$ cm

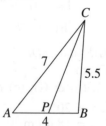

5. (a) 7   (b) 144°
6. (a) $x = 12$, $y = 18$ (b) (i) $\triangle DEC$ (ii) 4

Section B

1. (a) $2 + 6 + 10 + 14 + 18 + 22 = 72 = 2 \times 6^2$
   (b) 200   (c) $p = 16$, $q = 62$ (d) $2 \times (n + 1)^2$
2. (a) (i) 32   (ii) 3 even numbers, 2 odd numbers
   (b) $3\,000
3. (a) 136   (b) 0.013 m^3 (c) 1.768 m^3 (d) $981.24
4. (a) 18 cm   (b) (i) $x = 117°$, $y = 79°$ (ii) $x = 112°$, $y = 72°$
5. (a) 50   (b) 1 h 3 min

152